Classroom Instructional Tactics

Classroom Instructional Tactics

Evaluating Instruction

Expanding Dimensions of Instructional Objectives

W. James Popham

Eva L. Baker

PRENTICE-HALL, INC.
Englewood Cliffs, New Jersey

Classroom Instructional Tactics

W. James Popham

Eva L. Baker

Graduate School of Education

University of California, Los Angeles

74974

PRENTICE-HALL, INC.
Englewood Cliffs, New Jersey

Library of Congress Cataloging in Publication Data

POPHAM, W JAMES.
   Classroom instructional tactics.

   1. Teaching—Programmed instruction. I. Baker,
Eva L., Joint Author. II. Title.

LB1025.2.P628   371.1'02'177   72–8877
ISBN 0–13–136242–9
ISBN 0–13–136234–8(pbk.)

© **1973 by Prentice-Hall, Inc.**
Englewood Cliffs, N.J.

10 9 8 7 6 5 4 3 2 1

Printed in the United States of America

Prentice-Hall International, Inc., *London*
Prentice-Hall of Australia, Pty. Ltd., *Sydney*
Prentice-Hall of Canada, Ltd., *Toronto*
Prentice-Hall of India Private Limited, *New Delhi*
Prentice-Hall of Japan, Inc., *Tokyo*

Contents

v

Companion Audiovisual Materials

A set of filmstrip-tape instructional programs coordinated with the contents of this book is available from Vimcet Associates Inc., P.O. Box 24714, Los Angeles, California, 90024. Information regarding these materials is available upon request.

*Classroom
Instructional
Tactics*

Introduction

This book consists of a collection of six self-instruction programs designed to be completed individually by the reader. The focus of the book is on classroom instruction techniques. Each of the programs is intended to provide one or more tangible competencies which can be employed by a teacher in the design and conduct of classroom instructional activities. The skills provided by the programs should be of considerable value to individuals who are preparing for a teaching career in any level of instruction, kindergarten through college. Many experienced teachers will also find that the topics treated in the programs bear upon practical classroom decisions they must make regarding their instruction. Thus, both preservice and inservice teachers should profit from completing these programs.

Organization of the Book

The substance of these six self-instruction programs is briefly presented below:

WRITTEN PLANS FOR CLASSROOM INSTRUCTION. This program describes recommended elements for the two most

1

popular forms of classroom instructional plans, that is, the teaching unit and the lesson plan. The reader is given practice in identifying procedures which are either appropriate or inappropriate for lesson plans and teaching units.

INDIVIDUALIZING INSTRUCTION. By attempting to familiarize the reader with alternative ways of devising instruction so that it is attentive to the individual learner, this program offers a teacher several ways of individualizing classroom instruction. The most popular systems of individualizing instruction are examined along with specific instructional procedures suitable for large group instruction, small group instruction, and independent study.

INSTRUCTIONAL TACTICS FOR AFFECTIVE GOALS. Operating on the assumption that affective instructional goals are perhaps the most important which classroom teachers can accomplish, this program describes the general nature of three instructional tactics which are particularly useful for promoting the attainment of affective goals. Specifically, the reader is presented with the following three tactics: modeling, contiguity, and reinforcement, and is given practice in identifying when they are being employed by fictitious teachers.

THE TEACHING OF READING. This program describes an empirical model applied to the improvement of reading instruction. The reader practices describing the model, identifying examples of reading objectives and activities which illustrate the use of the model, and writing test items which measure reading skills that might be promoted by such an empirical model.

OPENING CLASSROOM STRUCTURE. This program examines the possibility of devising classroom activities that are less constricting than is so often the current case. Suggestions are offered for instructional plans which produce a more open classroom structure. Attributes of open structure for particular classroom situations are described.

DISCIPLINE IN THE CLASSROOM. This program describes a translation of operant methods to principles of classroom control. The reader learns to describe the basic rules of contingency management, to identify instances in which operant methods are being used, and to select solutions to common classroom problems according to a reinforcement paradigm.

Use of the Book

Since these programs are self-instructional, it is probable that you will be proceeding individually at your own pace. Incidentally, it is usually better to complete a whole program at a single sitting rather than to interrupt your work. Before commencing a particular program, first locate the answer sheet for that program (and detach it from the book if you wish). Then note the program's objectives and begin reading the textual material. On the answer sheet, write your responses to the questions posed in frames. After you have made the response, check the accuracy of your answer by reading further in the program. Preferably, you should respond in writing, although if you wish you may answer mentally. So that you do not inadvertently read too far and see the correct answer before making your response, wide bars like the one below have been inserted throughout the program.

The correct answers will appear immediately following the bar. When you see such a bar, mask off the section below it until you have made your response (a heavy answer mask has been provided inside the rear cover). *Then read on to discover the accuracy of your answer.* When you have completed a program, take the mastery test for that program and subsequently check your answers.

Several of the topics treated in these six programs are examined in more detail in the conventional nonprogrammed text, *Systematic Instruction,* also distributed by Prentice-Hall. Also available are related collections of self-instruction programs including *Planning an Instructional Sequence, Establishing Instructional Goals,* and *Evaluating Instruction.*

When you are ready, begin the first program.

Written Plans for Classroom Instruction

Objectives

In this program two common types of written plans for classroom instruction are described—namely, the teaching unit and the lesson plan. Recognizing that individual teachers will vary considerably in the way they use both of these plans, elements of each form are recommended but are, in a sense, only suggestive. While wishing to encourage teachers to devise written instructional plans, one is loath to urge that teachers give such detailed attention to planning that they turn completely from such planning. In general, the recommended elements for lesson plans and teaching units encourage the instructional planner to attend to the question "What do I want the learners to become?" rather than the question "What shall I [the teacher] do?"

Specifically, the objectives of the program are these. At the end of the program the reader will be able to:

1. Correctly use the terminology associated with lesson and unit planning by matching key terms with different paraphrase definitions of those terms.
2. List the recommended elements which should be included in teaching units.
3. List the recommended elements which should be included in lesson plans.
4. Decide whether given operations should be carried out in developing (a) lesson plans, (b) teaching units, (c) both, or (d) neither.

6

Unquestionably there are teachers who can conduct an inspiring class session without any planning whatsoever. But

aside from these fortunate few, most instructors find it impossible to base their day-to-day classroom efforts on spontaneity. Almost all teachers must plan in advance what will occur in the classroom.

In some ways this is highly desirable. By writing out their instructional plans prior to teaching, most teachers can become far more systematic than they would be by relying on "spur of the moment" decisions. Also, it is possible to survey a written plan carefully according to whatever criteria the teacher thinks important; unwritten plans, such as those carried "in the teacher's head," cannot be systematically appraised.

In this program the two most common types of written plans for classroom instruction will be described. These two, the teaching unit and lesson plan, should cover almost all instructional planning requirements of the classroom teacher. By mastering these two forms of written instructional plans, you should be able to design instructional sequences which, through careful consideration prior to and after implementation, should become markedly more effective.

Let's first examine some of the more common terms used in connection with written instructional plans. Although most educators have similar understandings of what these expressions mean, there are frequently different interpretations given in different school districts. Accordingly, it will be wise to do a little term-defining at the outset.

First, a *teaching unit.* A teaching unit is a plan of instruction extending over more than a single class period. A teaching unit could cover as short a span of time as two classroom periods or as long a span of time as an academic year. Most teaching units, however, are limited to a few weeks or a few months at most. For example, an English teacher might plan a four-week unit on "The Short Story," or a first grade teacher might design a six-week unit in reading on "word attack skills." Teaching units are usually organized around themes, problems, or particular skills the learners should acquire.

A *lesson plan* is a plan of instruction for a single class period. A history teacher might devise it on Monday for his Tuesday

class. An elementary teacher in a self-contained classroom has a choice of preparing separate lesson plans for different subjects, such as social studies, mathematics, reading, etc., or of preparing one expanded lesson plan for the entire day.

A *course of study* is a document, often prepared by the school district office rather than an individual teacher, which describes the content and sometimes the objectives to be treated in particular courses at particular grade levels. For instance, there might be a course of study dealing with tenth-grade biology at that grade level plus the topics to be treated during the year. Sometimes courses of study are highly pre-scriptive, that is, they allow a teacher few alternatives regarding the general topics to be treated. Other courses of study offer considerable latitude to the teacher in the selection of topics. Terms which are often used interchangeably with course of study are *syllabus* and *curriculum guide.*

Finally, the *resource unit* is a collection of *suggested* activities, resources, etc. which is designed to aid the teacher in preparing his own teaching unit. Resource units are usually prepared at the district office by groups of teachers or supervisory personnel and often consist of excellent alternatives from which the teacher can select.

To give you some practice in using these terms, here are a few descriptions as practicing teachers might phrase them. On your answer sheet indicate what the teacher is referring to by writing either the phrase *teaching unit, lesson plan, course of study,* or *resource unit.* For this first description, answer next to Number 1.

1.
"The objectives in this guide are too vague. I'm expected to plan for the whole year in my social science class and I can't tell what I'm supposed to cover."

Undoubtedly, this teacher was referring to a course of study.

Now answer next to Number 2 for the following exercise.

2.

"This is a detailed outline of what I will be doing and what my pupils will be doing on next Monday, fifth period."

You should have written lesson plan.

Answer next to Number 3 for the next exercise.

3.

"In planning daily arithmetic activities for my second grade pupils, I found this collection of possible topics, learner activities, and references most helpful."

The correct answer here is resource unit.

Now answer next to Number 4 for the following description.

4.

"This represents the best plan I've ever developed for teaching my civics class about 'local government.' It looks like a productive three-week session."

This instructor was clearly referring to a three-week teaching unit.

Before turning to a more detailed examination of teaching units and lesson plans, it should be noted that neither of these instructional plans need be developed in isolation by a single teacher. If there is a teaching team involved, or if the teacher can work with one or more colleagues, the quality of the resulting plans might be even better than if they had been developed alone.

Now, let's consider the teaching unit as a vehicle for organizing instructional plans. What should a teaching unit contain, and how should a teacher go about preparing one? In the following list are seven elements which many curriculum authorities believe all teaching units should contain.

Recommended elements in a teaching unit:
1. Precise instructional objectives
2. Pretest
3. Day-by-day activities
4. Criterion check
5. Posttest
6. Resources
7. Back-up lesson

Examine this list carefully, for sometime later you will be asked to reproduce it.

Recalling that the teaching unit usually covers several weeks' worth of instruction, the first thing the teacher should ascertain is whether there is a course of study which has certain requirements regarding the available time, topics to be treated, etc. Perhaps the local school faculty has agreed to emphasize certain points in the unit under consideration. There may even be state legislation which requires certain emphases. By first checking to see whether such curriculum constraints exist, the teacher will have a better idea of the options available to him.

The first things that go into a teaching unit are the instructional objectives to be accomplished during the time covered by the unit.

THE INSTRUCTIONAL
PLANNER SHOULD
DETERMINE WHETHER
THERE ARE ANY
CURRICULAR CONSTRAINTS.

Recommended elements in a teaching unit:
1. *Precise instructional objectives*
2.
3.
4.
5.
6.
7.

It is at this very early point that most teachers will have to struggle against an erroneous tendency which will crop up time and again during their instructional planning. They will want to focus on the question, "What should I do?" rather than on the question "What do I want the learners to become?" This is based on a straightforward distinction between ends and means. Which of these two questions is directed primarily toward ends and which toward means? Write either *ends* or *means* on your answer sheet next to Number 5.

5.
Question A: "What should I do?"
Question B: "What do I want the learners to become?"

You should have labeled Question A as one of means and Question B as one of ends.

Many beginning teachers are so concerned with what they will do and what they will have their students do that they focus immediately on what kinds of things will go on in the classroom. This is a mistake. There is a time to make decisions regarding what goes on in the classroom, but that is definitely not the first thing to be considered. *Only after making decisions about the kinds of modifications he is trying to promote in the learner's behavior should a teacher be concerned with instructional activities.*

And it is by specifying instructional objectives—as explicitly as possible—that the unit planner decides what he wants to have happen to the learners. The procedures for stating objectives properly have been treated elsewhere in considerable detail. For our purpose here, it will be sufficient to remind you that to be useful in making instructional decisions, the objectives for the unit must be described in terms of what the learner does or is able to do after the unit that he does not or cannot do before the unit. That is, *all* of the teaching unit's objectives should be stated in operational or measurable terms.

Some teachers may find it helpful to organize their specific objectives around a few more general goals which are not behaviorally stated. This is quite acceptable as long as the general goals are operationalized by subsequent statements of explicit goals.

Which, if any, of these objectives, for example, is properly stated for purposes of an instructional unit? Answer next to Number 6 by circling the letter of any operationally stated goals.

6.
A. The teacher will cover the background of the U.S. Constitution.
B. Pupils will be able to understand the forces influencing the main elements in the Constitution.
C. Pupils will be able to identify the section of the Constitution at issue in hypothetical descriptions of Supreme Court decisions.

Only objective C is stated properly. Objective A refers to teacher, not pupil, activity, and objective B hinges on the meaning of the ambiguous term "understand."

Once all objectives have been tentatively listed for the unit, the teacher should probably inspect them qualitatively. Are there too many cognitive objectives of a low level nature? Are there any objectives which deal with affective dimensions of learner behavior? Can the objectives realistically be accomplished in the time available?

The second recommended element in a teaching unit is a pretest based on the objecives.

> Recommended elements in a teaching unit:
> 1. Precise instructional objectives
> 2. Pretest
> 3.
> 4.
> 5.
> 6.
> 7.

A good pretest will cover all objectives and any prerequisites or entry behaviors which the teacher feels must be possessed by the learners in order to achieve the objectives. A *complete* version of the pretest, preferably keyed to objectives, should be included in the unit. This pretest should be administered at the very beginning of the unit, for student performance on it may dictate modifications in the previously selected objectives. What if your class can already perform some of the behaviors you are trying to promote? Obviously, you should not teach pupils things they can already do, so such goals would have to be altered or deleted.

In review, which one of these pretests would be most suitable? Circle the correct answer to Number 7.

7.
A. A largely unstructured essay exam to get a general idea of what students know.
B. Items covering all objectives plus requisite entry behaviors.
C. Items covering only instructional objectives.

You should have selected pretest *B.*

The third recommended element in a teaching unit is a day-by-day description, in general terms, of the activities to be carried out during the unit.

> *Recommended elements in a teaching unit:*
> 1. Precise instructional objectives
> 2. Pretest
> 3. *Day-by-day activities*
> 4.
> 5.
> 6.
> 7.

As we shall see in our consideration of lesson plans, there is a place for extremely precise descriptions of what should happen in the classroom—but that place is not in the unit. It is too difficult to make exact time estimates a week or more in advance. Unpredictable classroom occurrences will muck up your predictions. Thus, the following description for one day during the planned teaching unit would be acceptable.

> *Tuesday, 2nd week:* Discuss reading assignment in class; students choose panel discussion topics; description given of steps in planning panel reports; students make preliminary plans in groups.

Several days may be essentially the same in this kind of plan, so, if it would be easier to state something like this, it too would be acceptable:

> *Third week, Monday through Thursday:* Students spend 1/3 period going over homework exercises; concept for each day's topic explained 1/3 period; practice exercises with immediate feedback conclude each day.

This is the time, of course, when the teacher should be concerned with what he does and what the students should do. By knowing what his goals are, he can select relevant learning activities, and he should, of course, capitalize on as many instructional principles as possible in designing the unit's day-by-day activities.

> *Recommended elements in a teaching unit:*
> 1. Precise instructional objectives
> 2. Pretest
> 3. Day-by-day activities
> 4. *Criterion check*
> 5.
> 6.
> 7.

The next recommended element in the unit is unique. It is referred to as the *criterion check* and consists of a check of the students' ability to accomplish the criterion behaviors *prior to the close of* instruction. Too many times a teacher only finds out during the unit's final examination that the instruction has not been effective. The use of a criterion check permits the teacher to gauge how well the learners are proceeding while he still has time to do something about it.

The criterion check is sort of a short version posttest. But since it is to be used for your purposes in possibly modifying your instructional tactics, not for grading the pupils, all students need not complete the same test. This check involves the use of *item sampling* whereby short tests, maybe covering only one or two objectives, are given at random to only a few students in the class. In a short time the teacher can get an idea of how well the whole class is doing. In much the same way (insofar as results on the pretest and posttest are to be used for the teacher's instructional decisions, not for assigning grades) item sampling is a useful technique for pre- and posttesting.

A critical element in a teaching unit is the posttest, which covers all behaviors described in the objectives.

> *Recommended elements in a teaching unit:*
> 1.   Precise instructional objectives
> 2.   Pretest
> 3.   Day-by-day activities
> 4.   Criterion check
> 5.   *Posttest*
> 6.
> 7.

Which of the following assertions do you think is more defensible regarding the nature of the posttest? Answer next to Number 8 on the answer sheet.

8.
A. The posttest can consist of any kind of behavioral assessment, not just paper and pencil items.
B. The posttest should consist exclusively of paper and pencil test items, preferably those which can be objectively scored.

You should have circled *A*. It is highly unlikely that all worthwhile objectives can be measured through the use of paper and pencil items. Indeed, one can think of behaviors in the affective domain which might be revealed by the volitional behavior of learners in a subsequent course, a course not even taught by the instructor who is planning the unit. Hence, "posttest" in the sense we are using it is not equivalent to "final examination" but, instead, covers a wide range of behaviors.

Recommended elements in a teaching unit:
1. Precise instructional objectives
2. Pretest
3. Day-by-day activities
4. Criterion check
5. Posttest
6. *Resources*
7.

A sixth element recommended for inclusion in a teaching unit is a list of all references to be used, for example, texts, films, audio tapes, etc. Any item which the students must have should be listed, probably at the end of the unit. If possible, a coding scheme should be used, for example, Resource # 1, # 2, etc., so that these items can be readily referred to during the day-by-day description section.

Finally—and this may be more important for beginning teachers than for experienced teachers—it is recommended that each unit contain one or more "back-up" lessons which may be used by the instructor in case of some instructional emergency.

> *Recommended elements in a teaching unit:*
> 1. Precise instructional objectives
> 2. Pretest
> 3. Day-by-day activities
> 4. Criterion check
> 5. Posttest
> 6. Resources
> 7. *Back-up lesson*

For example, suppose a scheduled film fails to arrive on time or some other required instructional materials are unavailable. What do you do then? It may be easy to proceed to the

next unit activity, or it may not be. A back-up lesson plan which can be thrown into the vacuum is comforting. The nature of the back-up lesson plan will depend on the subject and grade level, of course, but it should generally be directed toward an objective which is relevant to the unit's topic but which might not be covered in the time available. Back-up lessons can be used also if the teacher has seriously overestimated the time certain activities will take, or if pretest results indicate that many changes must be made in the unit's objectives and activities.

We have now examined seven recommended elements of a teaching unit. In the spaces provided by Number 9, see if you can list all seven without referring to the text.

These were the seven recommended elements.

Recommended elements in a teaching unit:
1. Precise instructional objectives
2. Pretest
3. Day-by-day activities
4. Criterion check
5. Posttest
6. Resources
7. Back-up lesson

The lesson plan is a far more detailed description of what is to take place in the classroom. In addition to the customary descriptive information such as the teacher's name, date, course, etc., a lesson plan should have the following five elements:

Recommended elements in a lesson plan:
1. Precise instructional objective(s)
2. Learner activities
3. Teacher activities
4. Time estimates
5. Assignments (if any)

Let's briefly examine each of these items. First, the behavioral objective or objectives for that particular lesson should be described. If the lesson plan is based on a teaching unit, it may be simpler to note "Unit objective four" than to rewrite the objective. Next, a description of what the learners are going to be doing during the period is necessary. For example, if pupils are to be reading silently for part of the period, then discussing their reading, be sure to list both activities. Next, the teacher's activities should be described: "Instructor discusses theorem, stressing relationship to previously examined theorems." Next, time estimates for each activity should be added, for example, "Discussion: 15 minutes." Obviously time estimates will not be completely accurate. Yet, such estimates are helpful in deciding how to use the minutes available in a class period. Finally, if there is an assignment, it should be listed, along with the due date.

To make it easier to incorporate these five features in your lesson plans duplicate some blank lesson plan forms which provide for each element. There is no single form for a lesson plan, simply use one that is easy for you. The following is a common form:

A Suggested Form for a Lesson Plan

Teacher's Name _____ Date _____ Period _____

Objective(s)_____

_____

Time	Teacher Activity	Student Activity

Assignment _____

The amount of detail that goes into a lesson plan should depend on the teacher's own preferences. It would be foolish to require so much detail that lesson planning would become aversive and the instructor might turn to "winging it" rather than planning. The general recommendation would be to use as much detail as you can until the planning starts to become aversive—then stop, quickly.

Now re-examine the five recommended elements of a lesson plan. When you are ready, see if you can list them next to Number 10 on the answer sheet without referring to the text.

Now check your answer with the list supplied above.

For some final practice, see if you can determine whether the following operations should be carried out in the preparation of teaching units, lesson plans, both, or neither. Circle the *TU* for teaching unit, the *LP* for lesson plan, the *B* for both, the *N* for neither. For this first item, answer next to Number 11.

11.
The instructional planner should state precise objectives in terms of learner behavior.

You should have circled *B*, since behavioral objectives are recommended for both teaching units and lesson plans.

Now answer next to Number 12 for the following exercise.

12.
A pretest must be included by the instructional planner.

You should have answered *TU*, for only in a unit is the pretest required. It would be silly to pretest every day. Many good lesson plans never have any testing in them. Examinations should be administered at appropriate times in the overall unit, not as a daily ritual. Answer next to Number 13 for the following item.

13.
The instructional planner should determine whether there are any curricular constraints.

Once this is acertained prior to preparing a unit, it need not be done prior to each lesson plan. You should have circled *TU*.

How about this next operation? Answer next to Number 14.

14.
The instructional planner should focus on the question: "What should I do?"

The correct answer is *N*. Although at times it must be raised, this is *never* the question on which to focus. Teachers must constantly guard against such a means-orientation to teaching. An ends-orientation is one which will produce better results in learners.

In summary, we have examined the two most common forms of written instructional plans for the classroom. By using them you can make more explicit your own instructional designs. Of course, the final test regarding whether your plans were effective rests on the degree to which your instructional objectives were achieved. Once these results are available, you can determine which elements of your plans should be retained or modified so that in the future they will facilitate more effective classroom teaching.

Individualizing Instruction

Objectives

The general goal of this program is to encourage educators to think more diversely about methods of providing instructional approaches which are attentive to the individual learner. Two basic vehicles are employed for this purpose. First, a distinction is drawn between individualizing objectives versus individualizing instructional procedures. Second, three school organizational patterns suitable for individualization are described and specific instructional procedures are suggested for each.

More explicitly, the program has three objectives. At the conclusion of the program the reader will be able to:

1. Distinguish between descriptions of individualized instruction based primarily on (a) individualized objectives, or (b) individualized instructional procedures.
2. List and briefly describe three school organizational patterns recommended for individualizing instruction.
3. Supply three or more specific instructional procedures suggested for use in (a) large group instruction, (b) small group instruction, or (c) independent study.

Almost all classroom teachers believe that instructional approaches which are attentive to the differences among individual learners will be superior to those schemes which are oblivious of such differences. Truly individualized education has for many teachers been a cherished, even if sometimes unattainable, goal. In recent years we have seen the introduction of various educational schemes which can contribute toward effectively individualizing instruction. This program will attempt to systematize some of these suggestions so that educators who wish to move toward more individualized instructional approaches will be able to consider an enlarged range of alternatives. We will examine two major methods of individualizing instruction, several school organizational patterns which are conducive to individualized approaches, and a number of specific instructional procedures which can be blended into an effectively differentiated system.

It is particularly important to distinguish between two basically different methods of making an educational system attentive to different individuals. We can individualize instruction either by providing differential educational *ends* or differential *means* of achieving those ends. We can, for exam-

INDIVIDUALIZED
ENDS

INDIVIDUALIZED
MEANS

ple, attempt to promote different objectives for different learners, thus individualizing the ends of instruction. On the other hand, we might have identical objectives for all students but try to vary our instructional procedures so that such procedures were more suited to different individuals, thus individualizing the means of instruction. For example, some pupils might learn better by discussions or similar oral approaches, while others might learn best from self-directed reading. We could individualize instructional means by providing both approaches for achieving a given set of objectives. To repeat, whenever we try to achieve *different objectives* for different students, we are individualizing instructional *ends;* when we try to use *different teaching tactics* to achieve the same objectives with different learners, we are individualizing instructional *means.*

Let's see if you can identify whether individualized instruction is present in some fictitious examples (if none, circle n) and, if it is, whether it represents individualizing instructional ends (e), means (m), or both (b). For this first example, circle the appropriate letter next to Number 1 on the answer sheet.

1.

Based on mid-year achievement test performances, Mrs. Gibbs decides to provide remedial instruction for some of her students and enrichment instruction for others.

Although it may be difficult to decide in this case, Mrs. Gibbs is probably individualizing instructional ends (e), for the students pursuing enrichment topics are undoubtedly aiming toward different objectives.

Here is an easier example. Decide whether individualized instruction is being employed here and, if so, whether it represents individualized ends, means, or both. Answer next to Number 2.

2.

Students in an advanced mathematics class can choose among three ways of getting ready for the final exam: (1) discussions with the teacher, (2) reading the text, or (3) completing a set of programmed instructional materials.

Here we see an instance of individualizing instructional means, for different instructional procedures are available to the learners.

How about the next exercise? Answer next to Number 3.

3.

Beyond a set of basic objectives stipulated by the teacher, students are allowed to select a minimum of three supplementary objectives each term. For all supplementary objectives at least two alternative methods are provided for the students.

This situation seems to reflect an attempt to individualize both ends and means. An optimally individualized instructional scheme would undoubtedly attempt to adapt both objectives and instructional procedures to the individual learner.

Answer this next exercise by Number 4 on the response sheet.

4.

Mr. Locksteppe starts a class session by having the students chant in unison the *Pledge of Allegiance to the County Curriculum Guide*. The pupils then listen as he lectures on the topic, "Procrustes, a hero for our times."

Clearly, Mr. Locksteppe is not individualizing his instruction. Teachers such as this probably consider it an outright concession when physical education classes differentiate between boys' and girls' dressing rooms. But, although in reality there are few teachers in our schools who hold Mr. Locksteppe's values, there are many teachers who, for all practical purposes, achieve the same results. Their classes are unglittering examples of routinized, undifferentiated instructional activity. Neither instructional objectives nor instructional procedures are adapted to individual differences among learners. Perhaps such teachers do not recognize the possibilities of at least modestly individualizing their instruction ends or means through *grouping* practices. In a sense, this relates to one's basic conception of what is involved in individualized instruction. In the abstract, an ideally individualized instructional system would be adaptive to *each* learner as a totally unique human being (Many educators have fondly contemplated the notion of a teacher sitting at one end of a log with a student at the other end). At the end of a full day of teaching five different classes with 35 pupils per class, some of these same teachers might prefer to *use* the log on a few students. Frankly, in most educational situations the possibility of devising an idiosyncratic instructional program for each learner is unrealistic. But we can usually make *some* adaptations to different learners via grouping practices. Suppose, for example, that a teacher recognized that a proportion of his class was already familiar with a given topic, while for the rest of the students the topic was new. As a minimum effort, he might provide a different objective for the already knowledgeable group. Even such two-group differentiation can be legitimately considered as individualizing instruction. That it isn't the best individualization is obvious. That it's better than nothing should be equally obvious.

Sometimes the chief deterrent to individualizing instruction is the rigid organizational structure of the school's operational program. All classes are exactly 55 minutes in length; stu-

dents are assigned to classes or grade levels on the basis of
their chronological age; and each teacher holds forth in one

ACHTUNG, ACHTUNG!!
IN PRECISELY 9 MINUTES
ALL PUPILS WILL MARCH,
NOT WALK, TO THEIR
PERIOD TWO CAGES....

classroom. Such patterns do not preclude individualized instruction, for differentiation can be accomplished even within
such constraints. There are, however, several patterns for organizing a school's operations which, by their very nature,
tend to encourage individualized instruction. We shall examine the three most widely advocated of these school organizational patterns.

TEAM TEACHING. During the past decade a great deal of
attention has been given to *team teaching* as an organizational scheme to stimulate individualized instruction. Although there are almost as many ways of structuring team
teaching as there are teaching teams, certain characteristics
are common to most team teaching approaches. First, there
are multiple teaching personnel, which means a teacher will
be teamed with other teachers of equal status and responsibilities or differentiated status and responsibilities. Secondly,

a larger than customary group of students will be instructed by the teaching personnel. Finally, there will typically be supplementary paraprofessional personnel, such as student teachers or clerical assistants, to aid the instructional staff. Because of the possibilities of more flexibly arranging interactions between teachers and pupils, team teaching approaches generally foster individualization of instruction. For example, while one teacher instructs the bulk of the students in a large lecture situation, other teachers can be working with the remaining pupils in small group remedial or enrichment sessions. Teaching teams have been tried in almost every conceivable instructional situation, often with fine results. Nothing inherent in a team teaching approach insures that it will yield effectively differentiated instruction. If the instructional team members are incompatible, or if they are unwilling to expend the necessary energy to plan for differentiated instruction, team teaching can fail catastrophically. If properly implemented, however, its potential for individualized instruction is enormous.

NONGRADED PROGRAMS. A second organizational pattern used to encourage individualization is the *nongraded pro-*

NON-GRADED PROGRAMS

gram. Nongraded instructional approaches eliminate conventional grouping of students into arbitrary grade levels by chronological age. Rather, students of different chronological age are grouped together according to their accomplishments. In basic skill subjects, such as mathematics, nongraded programs permit the learner to make continuous progress as he sequentially masters a series of well-identified objectives. Nongraded programs, by their very nature, almost shriek for individualization. It is difficult to imagine a reasonably well devised, nongraded program in which differential instruction was not present. Of course, this school organization pattern is as susceptible as any to inadequate administration. In some nongraded schools chaos seems to be just around the corner. Yet, as with team teaching, nongrading offers great promise for individualization.

FLEXIBLE SCHEDULING. A third organizational pattern receiving considerable attention is flexible scheduling. In contrast to organization of the school day into six or seven 50-minute periods, flexible scheduling permits a school's daily schedule to be more readily modified for different instructional purposes. Employing a term borrowed from architecture, the school day is divided into *modules,* usually about 20 minutes in length, which can be used singly or in combination. Classes may meet for any number of modules per day or per week, depending on the instructional requirements. Few classes meet for only one module, but many meet for two, three, or four per day, some laboratory classes meet even for five or six. Generally, 15–25 modules comprise a school day, so that it is quite common to have a student enrolled for eight or more classes. Some classes begin and end while others are continuously in session. The bookkeeping requirements of a flexible scheduling organizational pattern are considerable, of course. Hence, use of a computer-based monitoring system is often advocated. As can be seen, however, flexible scheduling permits far greater attention to the individual learner's instructional requirements. We have examined then,

three school organization patterns designed to foster individualized education, both individualization of ends as well as
means. Review them briefly, for in a moment you will be
asked to list them.

> *Organizational patterns conducive to individualized in-
> struction:*
> 1. Team teaching
> 2. Nongraded programs
> 3. Flexible scheduling

Now, without referring to the list, see if you can recall these
three patterns by listing them beside Number 5 on the answer sheet.

5.
Organizational patterns conducive to individualized instruction:

(1) _____

(2) _____

(3) _____

Your answer should have included these three patterns:

> *Organizational patterns conducive to individualized in-
> struction:*
> 1. Team teaching
> 2. Nongraded programs
> 3. Flexible scheduling

But these three patterns appear to require a rather thorough
reorganization of a conventional school's operations. Do you
think any elements of these three patterns could be incorpo-
rated by one teacher restricted to a single classroom? Answer Yes or No next to Number 6.

An optimistic and correct response is yes. While there are clearly limitations in one teacher's trying to devise individualized instructional approaches for a single classroom, some features of these three organizational plans might prove useful. For example, drawing from team teaching approaches, an instructor might enlist the aid of several advanced students in his class, having them teach some of the other students while the teacher worked in specialized ways with smaller numbers of pupils. From nongraded approaches the teacher might use limited conceptions of nongrading even within a single class, particularly the central notion allowing the students to make continuous progress through the course. From flexible scheduling, it might be possible to organize even a regular classroom period into more rearrangeable modules of 15–20 minutes duration.

Normally, individualized instructional schemes will be organized around three general instructional approaches: large group instruction, small group instruction, and independent study, for in order to individualize instructional objectives, the teacher must employ a range of different instructional procedures. To illustrate, suppose a teacher relies exclusively on a total group lecture-discussion approach. Even if certain students are permitted to pursue different objectives, it is difficult to see how such learners could work toward dissimilar objectives unless there are several instructional approaches available so that, even if split into only two groups, different students can be doing different things at the same time. The chief limiting factors in individualizing instruction are characteristically the teacher's imagination and energy. Thus, it is important to increase the range of specific instructional procedures within the teacher's repertoire, so that in conjuring up individualized instructional schemes, either of ends or means, a teacher can choose among numerous alternatives. In turn, we'll examine several instructional procedures particularly useful for large group instruction, for small group instruction, and for independent study. Let's look first at four procedures well suited to large group instruction.

For large group instruction:
1. Instructional lectures
2. Guest speakers
3. Elaborate demonstrations
4. Group-paced media presentations

LARGE GROUPS. Perhaps the *lecture* is the most widely used classroom instructional procedure. If well planned and well delivered, teacher-presented lectures can be particularly effective for use with large groups.

Guest speakers often can be profitably employed during an instructional sequence because of their special expertise or personal experiences. To make optimal use of guests' limited time, they can be used in speech-like settings with as many pupils as possible.

Another time large group instruction seems warranted is when elaborate *demonstrations* are either quite costly or take much preparation time. For instance, if a complicated science experiment involves several hours of set-up time, then it makes sense to have many students view the experiment at the same time.

A fourth technique particularly suitable for large group instruction involves the use of *group-paced media* such as films, audio tapes, or sound-filmstrip programs. For instance, if a sound-filmstrip program is designed so that all learners must complete the program at a predetermined speed, then a large group of pupils can interact with the sound-filmstrip program as effectively as can a small group.

Of course, all four of these procedures can be employed also with smaller groups, in some instances very wisely, but possess elements which make them particularly suitable for large groups. Without referring to the text, see if you can recall at least three of these four techniques and list them, in any order, by Number 7 on the answer sheet.

7.
For large group instruction:
1. _____
2. _____
3. _____
4. _____

You should have identified three or more of these:

> *For large group instruction:*
> 1. Instructional lectures
> 2. Guest speakers
> 3. Elaborate demonstrations
> 4. Group-paced media presentations

The actual size of a large group is more dependent on physical facilities than any other factor. Many experienced teachers have indicated that up to 300 or 400 learners can be effectively accommodated in a large group. Seating facilities, public address equipment, and related physical arrangements are the critical considerations.

SMALL GROUPS. Turning to small group instruction, we can identify several instructional procedures designed to capitalize on the reduced size of the learner group. Again, the actual sizes of small groups can be varied: many teachers prefer 8–10 pupils, but agree that 12–15 can be involved if necessary.

For small group instruction:
1. Discussions
2. Cooperative projects
3. Laboratory activities
4. Subgroup presentations

The real value in small group work is that no pupil can avoid involvement in the learning process. The reticent student who can, in effect, withdraw from a class of 35 children finds it harder to hide when only ten pupils are involved. Quite naturally, therefore, *discussions* are an extremely effective instructional procedure to use with small groups. The teacher (or whoever is responsible for the discussion) should realize that careful planning is required for a productive discussion; only rarely do good discussions emerge spontaneously without background preparation from the participants and careful questions designed by the instructor. A second technique which can be wisely used with small groups involves *cooperative projects* in which the entire group must work together on some collective enterprise. For example, a group of learners might undertake a research project in which different members of the group take responsibility for varied assignments such as a library search, data-gathering, writing, group coordination, etc.

A variant on the second technique is the use of *laboratory activities,* commonly seen in science courses. During laboratory activities, learners often work alone or in pairs; but, since the work proceeds within the limits of a group defined activity, there are ample opportunities for interaction among well-known acquaintances.

A fourth possibility involves *subgroup presentations,* such as panel discussions, debates, or symposiums, by a few of the group members—perhaps only three or four. These presentations can be made either within the small group itself or to another small group. Ideally, a discussion following the presentation can capitalize on the reduced group size and the heightened possibility for interaction.

See if you can recall at least three of the four instructional procedures suggested for use with small groups and list them beside Number 8 on the answer sheet.

8.

For small group instruction:

1. _____

2. _____

3. _____

4. _____

You should have identified three or more of these.

For small group instruction:
1. Discussions
2. Cooperative projects
3. Laboratory activities
4. Subgroup presentations

INDEPENDENT STUDY. We now will consider four instructional procedures which are generally recommended for the learner as he engages in independent study.

For independent study:
1. Commercial self-instruction materials
2. Teacher-developed self-instruction materials
3. Instructional resource centers
4. Tutoring programs

When the learner is working on his own, one immensely useful procedure is to have him work through *commercially prepared self-instructional materials*. Some of these will be programmed instructional materials, some will be workbooks, some will even be standard textbooks or other conventional books. The important thing is that the learner can work at these independently, at his own pace, without heavy reliance on an instructor. If the materials have really been designed to teach, rather than serve as information storehouses, all the better. More and more publishers are trying to develop instructional materials which, if used as directed, take responsibility for a student's learning. Such materials are ideal for an individualized instructional system.

If no commercial materials are available, an instructor may have to employ *teacher-developed self-instructional materials*. In the past few years, several forms for such teacher-prepared materials have become popular. For example, the UNI-PAC is a self-contained set of teaching and learning materials organized around measurable instructional objectives and designed to teach a single concept. Similarly, Learning Activity Packages (LAPs), developed by the Nova School in Fort Lauderdale, are organized around the attainment of measurable objectives. Both of these approaches attempt to systematize a teacher's efforts to develop effective self-study materials. If a teacher has time to prepare such materials, he can follow guidelines such as those associated with LAPs and UNIPACs.

A third suggested vehicle for promoting independent study involves *instructional resource centers*. An instructional resource center is a depository, clearing house, and administrative locus for materials and equipment needed by students as they engage in independent study. For example, commercially prepared and teacher-developed instructional materials are distributed through such centers. Hopefully, independent study carrels are also available in the center so that pupils may either work in the instructional resource center or take materials away for work elsewhere.

A fourth procedure for individual instruction involves *tutoring programs* through which individual students are tutored either by a classmate, an older student, or a paraprofessional such as a part-time district employee. Since they can be set up on a one-to-one basis, tutoring programs permit almost complete individualization. Those engaged in the tutoring, however, must be carefully trained to employ sound instructional practices. Too many tutorial programs have floundered merely because it was assumed that anyone, even without experience and training, could effectively tutor. If employed judiciously in a well-coordinated system of independent study, these four procedures should yield good results.

Without referring to the text, see if you can recall at least three of the four and list them next to Number 9.

9.
For independent study:
1. _____
2. _____
3. _____
4. _____

You should have identified at least three of these:

For independent study:
1. Commercial self-instruction materials
2. Teacher-developed self-instruction materials
3. Instructional resource centers
4. Tutoring programs

Now, using these three general approaches an instructor can devise an individualized instruction system as this:

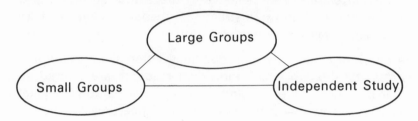

An Individualized Instruction System

The exact proportion of time to devote to any of these three elements is dependent, of course, on a particular instructional setting. The variations in emphasis can be enormous. There is nothing intrinsically superior about any of the three approaches, that is, it should not be assumed that the program with the greatest percentage of independent study is necessarily the best. As with all instructional schemes, we must evaluate the system in terms of the results it produces with learners. Are more learners achieving more worthwhile

goals? If so, then the individualization plan is worth the effort. Too many new converts to individualized instructional approaches become enamoured of these schemes for their own sake, never checking whether there are clear dividends for the learners.

Educational systems which make an effort to adapt both instructional objectives and instructional procedures to individual learners will promote far better results for most learners. Even so, those involved in devising these systems should be as attentive to evaluating the learner outcomes produced as they are to designing the mechanism by which they hope to individualize instruction. Individualized instruction should never become a fetish. It should become a *demonstrably* superior way of educating our learners.

Instructional Tactics for Affective Goals

Objectives

This program is designed to provide the reader with several instructional procedures of proven worth in modifying an individual's affectively oriented behavior. In general, the program emphasizes the importance of affective goals and considers a number of points related to the design of classroom instructional sequences.

More specifically, at the close of the program the reader will be able to:

1. Describe the general nature of each of the following instructional tactics: modeling, contiguity, and reinforcement.
2. Indicate which, if any, of these three instructional tactics are being employed when presented with fictitious descriptions of teachers attempting to accomplish affective objectives.

All across the nation each fall thousands of children start out for their first experience in a public school kindergarten with keen anticipation. *They want to go to school.* Most of them can't wait. It is impossible to forget the look of excitement on the face of such a child as the enthralling events of the school day are recounted that evening at dinner. And this feeling about school persists into the early years of school, for example, until the first and second grades. But soon thereafter we hear the same child yearning for vacations or wishing sickness would permit him to stay home from school. His

4th GRADE   KINDERGARTEN

attitude toward school has clearly become negative. We may have taught him to read, multiply, and spell, but we've often taught him to despise the process by which he acquired these skills. Yet, in the long run, a positive attitude toward learning may be the most important educational goal of all.

Hopefully, this type of incident will remind you that, in addition to modifying their intellectual skills—deliberately or inadvertently—teachers change children's attitudes, values, and feelings. Generally, these changes are referred to as *affective* changes and are contrasted with *cognitive* (intellectual) changes and *psychomotor* (physical skill) changes.

Many educators believe that the affective effects of instruction are profoundly more important than the cognitive or psychomotor skills which the schools produce. For instance, if a child's self-concept is damaged by unsuccessful interactions with arithmetic problems, the effects of such an affective change will be far more influential in later life than whether he can successfully engage in long division.

Similarly, the values learners develop during school regarding justice, tolerance, violence, citizenship, etc., are surely crucial outcomes of our educational enterprise. Certainly these affective dimensions are more critical than a student's ability to write a properly punctuated sentence or to type 40 words per minute.

Yet even though there is ample lip-service support for the importance of affective education in the schools, there are precious few systematic efforts on the part of teachers or school systems to promote the attainment of key affective

"MY CHILDREN NOT ONLY LEARN THEIR A,B,C's, THEY LEARN HOW TO BE FUNCTIONING MEMBERS OF TODAY'S DYNAMIC DEMOCRACY—AND TO MIND THEIR SNIPPY LITTLE TONGUES!"

goals. Although we *talk* about good citizenship and the promotion of proper values, we return to teaching cognitive skills and, occasionally, a psychomotor objective or two.

Now why does this preoccupation with cognitive goals predominate in our schools? Why do we give little attention to the attainment of affective objectives, even though most educators believe they are so crucial?

While numerous factors contribute to our almost total avoidance of systematic concern with affective education, two factors are perhaps most focal. Both considerations stem from the absence of two particular technical skills on the part of teachers.

First, most teachers are not able to specify instructional objectives of an affective nature in such a way that one can tell whether the objective has been achieved—that is, teachers are unable to operationalize their affective instructional goals in the form of *measurable* objectives.

Second, even if they are able to specify their affective instructional objectives with sufficient precision, most teachers do not possess a repertoire of instructional tactics particularly suited for such objectives. In short, they don't really know how to design an instructional sequence which is especially appropriate for attaining affective instructional goals. This instructional program will deal with the second of these two technical skills, that is, an ability to design instructional sequences which have a high probability of promoting the student's attainment of an affective objective.

> *Technical instructional skills needed for affective education:*
> 1. The ability to specify measurable affective objectives.
> 2. The ability to design instructional sequences which are appropriate for accomplishing such objectives.

We shall not concentrate on the first skill, specifying measurable affective instructional objectives; that topic is treated in another program in this series. Also, objectives bank agencies such as the Instructional Objectives Exchange* are now making available increasingly large collections of measurable objectives in the affective domain—collections from which educators can select those objectives and measures particularly appropriate for their own instructional situations. Thus, we shall concentrate on providing you with the skills necessary to put together a high quality affective instructional sequence once the objectives have been defined with sufficient clarity.

At the conclusion of the program you will be able to describe three instructional tactics to use in accomplishing affective goals and to identify situations in which each of the three tactics is being employed. Although the three instructional tactics are not magical, and must still be blended into an overall educational strategy which must be tried out and, if necessary, revised, sufficient research supports their efficacy that any teacher should become far more proficient by mastering them.

First, let's take a look at two instructional goals. Would the following instructional goals generally be conceded to be in the affective domain? Answer Yes or No by circling the appropriate answer on the response sheet by Number 1.

1.
A. The students will become more tolerant of individuals from socioeconomic strata other than their own.
B. Pupils will display more positive affect toward school as reflected by reduced absenteeism rates.

You should have answered Yes, for most people would agree that these two goals deal more significantly with the stu-

*Box 24095, Los Angeles, California 90024.

dent's attitudes, values, and feelings than with his cognitive skills. Of course, one may argue that there are no *exclusively* affective objectives, that is, goals with no admixtures of cognitive skills whatsoever, but we are concerned with the primary thrust of an instructional objective, and these two goals would appear to be legitimately classifiable as affective.

Which of these two goals lends itself better to a determination of whether the objective has been *achieved?* Circle the letter of the more measurable objective by Number 2 on the answer sheet.

You should have selected objective *B,* since it includes a critical ingredient missing in objective *A,* namely, a behavioral *indicator* of whether the objective has been achieved. Notice the phrase "as reflected by reduced absenteeism rates." Absenteeism rates are eminently measurable. We can calculate what proportions of school children are absent each month, or each week, or each day. And it is *imperative* that affective objectives, if they are going to do us much good instructionally, contain a behavioral indicator. If, as in objective *A,* the goal statement stops short of indicating the specific kind of behavior which will reflect goal achievement, then there is too much ambiguity regarding what the goal means. Notice in objective *A* that a hundred different interpretations could be given as to how the student might display the sought-for tolerance. Some of the interpretations would be reasonable; some would be indefensible. As the objective stands, we simply can't tell when the learner has achieved it.

You might be thinking that just because an affective objective statement includes a behavioral indicator does not mean the indicator is a valid one, that is, that the behavior truly reflects the affective dimension under consideration. You're quite right. Examine the following objective. Does it, in general, deal with an affective dimension? Answer Yes or No by Number 3.

3.
Students will manifest increased interest in the course subject matter by volunteering to give extra credit oral reports.

≡≡≡

You should have answered Yes; interest in subject matter is an affective consideration.

Is there a behavioral indicator included in the objective? Answer Yes or No next to Number 4.

≡≡≡

You should have responded Yes, for the phrase "by volunteering to give extra credit oral reports" clearly describes a learner behavior. But—and this is critical—do you think the behavioral indicator validly reflects the attainment of the affective goal in question? Answer Yes or No by Number 5 on the answer sheet.

≡≡≡

Even though the answer is not completely clear-cut, the best response here is undoubtedly *No*. It is likely that learners would be volunteering to give extra *credit* reports more to secure higher grades than to reflect genuine interest in the course.

The important lesson to learn from this illustrative objective is that while we may reject the legitimacy of the behavioral indicator, since we know precisely what it is, we can do just that—*reject it* and try to find a better one. Since affective goals are particularly elusive in some instances, we may often be obliged to use several less than totally satisfactory behavioral indicators and sort of "triangulate" on the affective goal in question.

As indicated earlier, a teacher must acquire skill in either generating or selecting affective instructional objectives which contain measurable indicators of goal achievement. This is critical, for the first step in designing an instructional sequence to accomplish an effective objective is to make certain the behavioral indicator or indicators of the desired goal is clearly spelled out. If it is not, then rework the objective until a measurable learner behavior is included.

> *Step One:* Make sure the affective instructional objective includes one or more behavioral indicators.

Once you have satisfied this initial requirement, you will see how inappropriate certain instructional tactics are which are quite suitable when used to attain cognitive instructional goals. For instance, look at the following objective.

> Learners will display a more positive attitude toward manual labor by securing higher scores on the *Kuder Vocational Interest Inventory.*

This appears to be a suitable affective objective, replete with a measurable behavioral indicator. One of the most useful teaching tactics for achieving *cognitive* goals is to give the learner appropriate practice, that is, practice in the behavior implied by the instructional objective. If we want to help children become good fraction dividers, we should give them lots of supervised practice in dividing factions. The principle of appropriate practice works very well for achieving cognitive goals. Would it work here? Do you think having students fill out the Kuder inventory every week would help achieve the objective? Probably not. We have to turn, instead, to instructional ploys particularly designed for achieving affective goals.

The three such tactics to be examined in the remainder of this program are *modeling, contiguity,* and *reinforcement.*

Three useful instructional tactics for the attainment of affective instructional goals:
1. Modeling
2. Contiguity
3. Reinforcement

First, let's examine *modeling* tactics. What are we trying to do when we employ modeling in an instructional sequence? In essence, we are attempting to get the child to learn by imitation. We are using the well-established principle that people do learn how to behave by watching others. All of us have acquired many of our personal ways of behaving by observing other people. Sometimes we were aware that we were patterning our behavior after others; often we weren't. Considerable high quality research indicates that modeling tactics can be very effective in modifying a learner's behavior. The teacher is really trying to provide a personal model for pupils so that they will emulate the behavior of the model. Sometimes the model will be the teacher himself. Sometimes the model can be another pupil or a visitor. But the model or models must display behavior which is consistent with the general affective goal involved.

For example, suppose a general affective objective in an elementary classroom was that the children would feel more positively about reading as displayed by an increase in their voluntary free reading behavior during optional-choice recess periods. With that kind of objective, would the following teacher employ a modeling tactic? Answer Yes or No next to Number 6 on the response sheet.

6.
Miss Thomas frequently tells her class, with considerable en-

thusiasm, about the interesting new novels she has been reading at home during the weekend.

You should have answered Yes. Miss Thomas is clearly modeling a behavior consistent with the affective goal she is seeking.

There are several considerations associated with modeling which the user of this instructional tactic must recognize.

First, effective use of modeling tactics by a teacher requires careful planning by that teacher. Sometimes highly suitable opportunities to display an appropriate model for the learners will arise without preplanning, but not often.

> Modeling situations should generally be planned in advance.

Second, for some objectives it is not necessary to model the exact type of behavior called for in the instructional objective as in the previous example where Miss Thomas was trying to model volitional reading behavior. It is often appropriate to model other behavioral indicators of the general affective goal sought than the explicit indicator cited in the objective. For many affective instructional goals there are numerous human behaviors which validly reflect attainment of the goal. For example, a teacher can display a love of classical music by all sorts of behaviors: going to concerts, buying stereo records, talking incessantly about Bach. A teacher can provide models of many such behaviors as a way of getting learners to adopt the general affective goal sought.

> The modeled behavior need not be equivalent to the behavioral indicator cited in the instructional objective as long as it is consistent with the affective goal sought.

Third, students learn better by imitation if, *in their view*, the model has prestige. Obviously, if the students do not esteem the teacher, they are unlikely to emulate his behavior. The more prestige the model has, the more likely that students will identify with him and imitate his behavior.

> A prestigious model is more effective.

Fourth, if students have seen the model rewarded for a particular kind of performance, they are more apt to engage in the rewarded behavior.

> Modeled behavior which is rewarded will be more apt to be adopted.

There are other nuances of modeling which the teacher may explore if he wishes to develop really high level skill in this tactic. In particular, he should consult the excellent research work of Professor Albert Bandura on this topic.

In review, modeling tactics involve the teacher's provision of models with whom the learners can identify and whose behavior they will imitate.

> Modeling tactics involve the provision of persons engaging in behavior which the learner can imitate.

Let's turn now to an examination of the use of *contiguity* tactics in promoting affective objectives. Briefly, contiguity tactics involve setting up appropriate conditions which are present whenever the learner is apt to associate the situation with the affective behavior sought. To illustrate, if we want the learner to like school, then we should arrange the school environment so that the conditions associated with school are as *positive* as possible. Seats should be comfortable, rooms should be attractively decorated, etc. Further, all *aversive* conditions should be removed if possible. Poorly ventilated rooms should not be used. Examination situations which are likely to promote embarrassment should be avoided.

The basic idea involved in contiguity tactics is to set up conditions contiguous with the learner's behavior which will be associated, in the way the teacher wishes, with the sought-for behavior. For instance, if we are attempting to *increase* a given learner response, then we should try to set up very positive conditions contiguous with the situations in which we hope the response will occur. If we are trying to *decrease* a certain learner response, then we would reduce the positive conditions and even might add some aversive conditions. Notice that we set up these conditions so that they are present irrespective of whether the student makes a particular response; that is, they are not rewards or punishments which are *contingent* on given learner responses. Instead, they are conditions designed to surround an activity and, in loose terms, be associated with that activity.

In general, an aversive condition is an event which causes the learner physical or mental discomfort. Aversive conditions include those which induce boredom, pain, frustration, anxiety, etc. Positive conditions are those which lead to increased self-esteem, confidence, pleasure, etc.

In this next example, decide whether the teacher is employing a contiguity tactic. If she is, answer Yes next to Number 7 on the response sheet. If not, circle No.

7.
Mrs. Bates wishes her students to feel more positive about people from other ethnic groups. She invites students from diverse ethnic groups in for frequent post-school parties which she tries to make as enjoyable as possible with games and refreshments.

You should have answered Yes, for Mrs. Bates is trying to set up positive conditions contiguous with her students' interactions with those from other ethnic groups. She should, of course, operationalize her goal more clearly by supplying a behavioral indicator of the desired positive feelings. Nevertheless, she is clearly employing a contiguity tactic.

In review, contiguity tactics require the instructor to provide positive or aversive conditions which, in view of the particular objective sought, will be associated by the learner with the behavior under consideration.

> Contiguity tactics involve arranging positive and aversive conditions so that they will be associated by the learner with the affective behavior sought.

Just as with modeling, contiguity tactics have to be carefully planned if they are to be effective. A teacher should decide systematically how to set up conditions so that they help students move toward desirable goals.

The third and last type of tactic to be considered is reinforcement. While somewhat similar to a contiguity tactic in that positive and aversive stimuli are involved, reinforcement has an important difference. Reinforcement tactics use positives and aversives in such a way that they are *contingent*, that is, dependent, on what the learner does.

Technically, there are two types of reinforcement ploys available to the teacher: positive reinforcement and negative reinforcement. Positive reinforcement adds a positive stimulus after a learner engages in a desired act. Negative reinforcement removes an aversive stimulus after a learner engages in a desired act. Note that both positive and negative reinforcement are designed to *increase* the probability of the learner's engaging in the response which they follow. Positive rein-

"IF YOU SPELL THESE 10 WORDS CORRECTLY, YOU GET AN ALL EXPENSE PAID TRIP TO DISNEYLAND!"

forcement is essentially the same as a reward. Negative reinforcement involves the withdrawal of a penalty.

Is positive or negative reinforcement being employed in this next situation? Answer by circling the R+ or R– next to Number 8 on the response sheet.

8.
A laboratory animal has been placed on an electrified grid which gives a mild shock until the animal presses a lever, whereupon the shock is discontinued. The animal's lever-pressing increases dramatically after a few such occurrences.

Negative reinforcement has been employed. The aversive stimulus, the shock, has been removed in order to increase the desired lever-pressing. Many educators confuse *punishment* with negative reinforcement. Punishment consists of *introducing* an aversive stimulus after an undesired response with the hope that the aversive stimulus will decrease the undesired response. Negative reinforcement requires the removal, not addition, of an aversive stimulus. In practice, however, because it's generally inhumane to set up aversive conditions just so that they can be removed, most teachers will employ positive rather than negative reinforcement. In some instances, however, an instructor may discover an existing aversive stimulus which may be removed in connection with a reinforcement tactic.

Is positive or negative reinforcement involved here? Answer next to Number 9.

9.
When his students display any behaviors which he believes to be reflective of a more positive attitude toward learning, Mr. Mack praises them.

This is an instance of positive reinforcement. The subject of how to use reinforcement techniques with sophistication in the classroom is beyond the scope of this program, but the enterprising teacher should investigate it in more detail. For example, you will learn that it is better to reinforce desired behaviors on an intermittent rather than constant schedule. You will also learn that in bringing about a desired behavior change it may be necessary to reinforce behaviors which are increasingly related to the desired behavior and, through such *successive approximations*, finally produce the desired behavior. In addition, you will discover that it is necessary to find out which things are reinforcing for which students. One pupil's perceived reward may be another's perceived punishment. Proper use of reinforcement tactics requires the teacher to individualize reinforcers for each pupil.

In review, reinforcement tactics consist of the teacher's use of positive or aversive stimuli *contingent* on the child's behavior. In general, positive reinforcers will be employed in most school situations where reinforcement tactics are used.

> Reinforcement tactics involve the introduction of positive stimuli or the removal of aversive stimuli after the student engages in a desired behavior.

Now let's give you some practice in discriminating between teachers using each of these three tactics. We'll start with some fairly simple exercises. In the following example, *one* of the three instructional tactics we have been discussing is employed. Decide which one and circle the appropriate letter next to Number 10 on the answer sheet. Is modeling (M), contiguity (C), or reinforcement (R) being used here

---

10.
This teacher observes her third-grade students as they interact and, whenever she sees any behavior which she believes is considerate of other people's rights, sends a brief note of commendation to the child's parents.

You should have circled the *R*, for this teacher is employing a reinforcement tactic. Now try this next exercise and decide whether modeling, contiguity, or reinforcement tactics are being used. Answer next to Number 11.

11.

This eleventh-grade government teacher frequently invites young, energetic politicians to her class so that they can describe their activities to the students. The teacher hopes to encourage more of her students to be interested in pursuing political careers.

═══════════════════════════════════════

For this exercise you should have selected modeling.

Try the following exercise and circle the letter of the appropriate tactic by Number 12 on the response sheet.

12.

Mrs. Gage wishes her students to like biology and has essentially redecorated and refurnished the school biology laboratory so that students will be working in attractive and comfortable surroundings.

═══════════════════════════════════════

This is an instance in which Mrs. Gage is employing a contiguity tactic. You should have circled the *C.* So much for the warm-up exercises. Let's try some more difficult discriminations. In each of the following fictitious accounts of teachers in action *one or more* of the three instructional tactics may be used. It is also possible that none may be used. Your task is to decide whether none, one, two, or three of these tactics are being employed. Answer by circling the appropriate letters. If none of the tactics is utilized, circle the *N.*

For the next exercise, answer beside Number 13 on the answer sheet.

13.

Mr. Brooks, an English teacher, tries to set an example of a person who can love poetry yet not be viewed by the students as "other worldly." He often reads poems to the class, interpreting them very sensitively. If any of his students report reading poetry on their own, he praises them lavishly.

For this exercise you should have circled the *M* and the *R*. Mr. Brooks is employing both modeling and reinforcement tactics, supplying the model himself and using praise as a reinforcer for those who behave as he wishes. Now try the next exercise and answer next to Number 14.

14.

John Garth, a physics teacher, wishes his students to become interested in physics. Because of his own status as the holder of an M.S. degree in physics, Mr. Garth believes the students will render his views the appropriate degree of respect. Accordingly, he often gives brief lectures on why today's youth should enjoy the study of physics.

Here is an instance where you should have circled the *N*. Mr. Garth is relying on exhortation, a ploy of dubious effectiveness, and is using none of the three tactics we have been analyzing.

For a final exercise try this next item and answer beside Number 15.

15.

Mr. Dee has so many entertaining things going on in his classes each day (word games, musical puzzles, treasure hunts, charades, good conversation) that when the end-of-period bell rings, his students almost have to be pushed out to go to their next class.

For this exercise you should have circled only the *C.* Mr. Dee appears to be relying on contiguity tactics.

In reviewing what we have seen in this program it should be clear that to blend these instructional tactics, and perhaps others, into an effective instructional strategy takes a lot of hard thinking on the part of the teacher. Good instructional designs for achieving affective goals do not often spring into being without the teacher's careful planning. But even when the teacher has devoted tremendous energy to the task of designing a sophisticated instructional plan for affective education, it has to be treated just like any other instructional plan—as an hypothesis to be tested out with learners. If, after

"PUPILS TODAY WE SHALL FIELD TEST EXPERIMENTAL LESSON PLAN AFFECT 209"

instruction, a sufficient number of learners display the behavioral indicator identified in the instructional objective, then the design was successful. If the objective was not achieved, then re-designing is warranted. For the skilled teacher realizes that in order to accomplish affective goals—and they are perhaps the most important goals we treat—considerable trial and revision will usually be needed. But when that first important affective objective is really achieved, when the teacher sees that a carefully devised instructional sequence can really work, that's all the reinforcement any teacher needs.

The Teaching
of Reading

Objectives

This program describes an empirical model applied to the improve-ment of reading instruction. The reader learns to describe the model and to identify examples of reading objectives and activities which illustrate the use of the approach. Practice is provided in writing test items which measure reading skills.

More specifically, at the conclusion of the program the reader should be able to:

1. Describe four rules used in the development of an empirical ap-proach to reading.
2. Identify objectives in reading which are operationally stated.
3. Identify activities which are most relevant for given objectives.
4. Write test items which match given objectives.

One of the most critical tasks of an elementary school teacher, or a secondary teacher who finds nonreaders in his class, is to teach children how to read. Many will flatly state that there is not much to teaching reading; a supply of flashcards, primers, and patience are sufficient. But in diverse areas of the country we are discovering that our children are *not* in fact learning to read. What is wrong with them? Or what is wrong with our reading instruction? When a child does not learn to read, what is the most probable cause? Circle the letter of the best answer next to Number 1 on the answer sheet.

1.
A.   He was not ready for reading and could not profit from instruction.
B.   The fault is in the instructional sequence.

While answer *A* is an enticing choice, usually the answer *B* is the case. The instruction in reading was not carefully planned.

Many teachers simply perform a routine set of behaviors and call themselves reading teachers. They show flashcards, separate children into reading groups, listen to the child reading aloud and congratulate themselves on a job well done. A careful analysis of what reading instruction is will show that such behavior patterns are wholly inadequate. Teachers rarely take the time to clarify, in their own minds, the goals of reading.

Which, if any, of the following statements could legitimately be considered as an objective of reading instruction? Circle the letter or letters of your answer by Number 2.

2.
A. The child will sound out newly encountered words.
B. The child will be able to tell what happened in the text he read.
C. The child will be able to pronounce all sounds of consonants in initial positions.

All three statements could be taken as goals of reading instruction; you should have circled all three letters. Because reading is so comfortable and familiar to most of us, we can fall into the error of assuming we know what the aims of our instruction are, when really we might have only the most general idea of what we mean by "reading."

To increase your impact as a teacher of reading, whether you are a first-grade teacher with a class full of beginning readers or a high school teacher with three nonreading adolescents, the first step is to describe fully your objectives. Is the next statement an adequate description? Answer by Number 3 on your answer sheet.

3.
The child will learn to read well.

Certainly the statement does one little good. The answer is No. All we know from it is that our concern is with reading rather than arithmetic.

What one must do is to analyze the task of "reading well" into components which can be carefully described. To be useful, these descriptions should be in terms of the child's observable behavior. Which of the following is an adequate description of a reading objective? Answer by Number 4.

4.
A. The child will finish Primer 1.
B. The child will be able to pronounce all words in Primer 1.
C. The teacher will present a four-week unit on Primer 1.

Choice *B* is the correct answer. Choice *A* does not clearly specify the competencies that the child will have acquired as a consequence of completing the primer. Choice *C,* because it focuses on teacher behavior, does not help in defining what the children will be able to do. In choice *B,* however, the child's observable behavior is described. The teacher could tell if the child had accomplished the objective by testing him. Determine which of these statements is an adequate statement of reading objectives. Answer by Number 5.

5.
A. The child will understand the story.
B. The child will demonstrate his ability with letter sounds.
C. The child will answer questions about the action of the story.

The correct answer is *C.* In choices *A* and *B* no explicit way for the child to demonstrate mastery was described. "Understanding," in choice *A,* could mean many different things and "ability with letter sounds," as in choice *B* could mean pronunciation, discrimination, or both. Thus the first rule for teaching reading is:

> *Rule One:* Describe anticipated objectives in behavioral terms.

Reading specialists disagree about what behaviors of children are critical to early reading success. On one hand, some experts define reading primarily in terms of comprehension. Behaviors extracted from this interpretation might be those in which the child is retelling the story in his own words, describing an alternate ending to the story, arranging pictures to show the sequence of events in the story, and so on.

Other reading specialists hold that early reading instruction should concentrate on the sound-symbol relationship. Behaviors appropriate to the decoding process might be that the child can say the sound of consonants, can give alternative sounds for vowels depending on their positions in given spelling patterns, can blend sounds together and smoothly pronounce new words.

There are arguments for both sides and, of course, neither position excludes the other. You might prefer an eclectic, behavioral definition of reading, and draw some observable competencies from the area of comprehension and some from the word attack area.

Regardless of your curricular position you should not proceed seriously in the teaching of reading until you have clearly stated your objectives.

See if you can recall, without referring to the text, the first rule in planning reading instruction. Answer next to Number 6 in the space provided.

You should have answered that the anticipated objectives must be described in behavioral or measurable terms.

The reason for the emphasis on objectives is twofold. Without clear descriptions of desired outcomes, it is difficult to plan profitable classroom experiences. Second, without stated goals, the evaluation of your instruction will be impossible.

Rule Two: Provide practice for *all* objectives.

The planning of classroom activities relevant to objectives will be considered first. If a teacher has in mind the skills desired for his pupils, he can systematically choose classroom activities designed to accomplish his objectives by employing rule two. As obvious as this position sounds, it is done all too rarely in classrooms across our country. Teachers may simply allow the sequence of a basal reading series to preempt their instructional decision making. They divide the children into three reading groups, largely on intuitive criteria, rarely check the progress of the children beyond the global behavior of "reading," and almost never reconstitute their reading groups. The consequence of this brand of instruction is that the bright children learn rapidly to read well, the average ability children struggle along for a while and then more or less succeed, and many of the less able children or those with language problems never learn to read at all. It is likely that the same distribution of reading success with this type of instruction would have occurred *without any instruction at all.* The bright children learn intuitively, probably without the teacher. The problem children barely learn anything, so they certainly don't profit much from the teacher's presence. The average children may or may not learn to read as a function of the teacher's action.

Do you think such instruction represents an efficient system? Answer Yes or No by Number 7.

You undoubtedly answered No. The alternative to this approach depends on the prior statement of objectives. Then the teacher can rationally select activities particularly designed to promote pupil learning in clearly identifiable ways. Suppose your objective was: "The child can sound out new words." By Number 8, mark Yes if the described activity efficiently aids in the achievement of that objective, No if it does not.

8.

Objective: The child can sound out new words.

Activity: The child will read aloud from his book in his reading group.

You should have answered No. While it is likely that in the course of reading the child may encounter new words, the activity described does not provide substantial practice on the desired objective. An activity which required children only to practice sounding out unfamiliar words would have been preferable.

For the next objective, circle *A* or *B* by Number 9 for the activity which provides the best practice.

9.
Objective: The child will be able to pronounce irregularly spelled words.
Activity A: The child practices sounding out many kinds of words.
Activity B: The child practices saying given irregularly spelled words.

You should have circled *B.* It would only confuse a child to expect him to sound out words which aren't spelled regularly. He would end up saying po-l*i*ce instead of po-leese.

By Number 10, circle *A* or *B* for the activity which provides the best practice for the following reading objective.

10.
Objective: The child will be able to say the sounds /d/ and /p/ in the presence of printed letters.
Activity A: The child is presented with *d* and *p* flashcards and is asked to pronounce the sounds.
Activity B: The child is given a sheet with *d*'s and *p*'s on it. When the teacher pronounces a sound, the child is to circle the symbol representing it.

You should have circled *A.* Unfortunately, many teachers give practice such as described in activity *B,* sound-to-symbol discrimination, without ever giving practice such as that described in activity *A.* While discrimination practice may be very valuable, the child must have the opportunity to actually make the sounds himself or there is little chance he will learn to do so at all. Data support the fact that opportunity to practice discrimination, such as circling *d*'s and *p*'s, without practice in making these sounds, will tend to result in lower pupil performance on both discrimination and pronunciation.

Identification of useful activities for practice should give you the idea that the typical menu of seatwork and reading aloud in static reading groups is not sufficient for the diverse objectives which could be properly described as "reading." Reading groups and seatwork are fine but are all too limited for the child who does not immediately understand how one learns to read. Specific activities related to clearly explicated objectives are necessary. You should feel encouraged to break away from what you have been doing and to try allowing for practice situations much closer to the objectives you have identified. You may have to reorganize your class so subgroups of pupils practice those skills in which they are deficient. Perhaps the traditional order of content presentation may have to be changed. For example, you may wish to delay the teaching of the alphabet until children have first learned to associate sounds with printed symbols. You might also choose to teach only small letter names, reserving the capital letters for later in the year. Teachers of remedial reading at the secondary school level will have to engage in similar schemes.

None of these suggestions is meant to be prescriptive. The point is that you can experiment; you can test which procedures for which objectives work for you. The most efficient way for *you* to teach reading is an empirical question. But almost nothing is to be gained by adhering to old models of behavior, particularly when most available evidence does not indicate that those models are successful.

For the following objective, mark which activity provides the best opportunity to practice the described behavior. Answer next to Number 11.

11.

Objective: The student can pronounce newly encountered regularly spelled words.

Activity A: The student, when given a word pronounced by the teacher, can sound the word into its phonemic parts.

Activity B: The student, when given a printed word, can sound it out and pronounce it.

Activity *B* is the correct choice. Practice allowed the children must provide the chance for them to perform the exact behavior stipulated in the objective.

For this next question, answer by Number 12 and circle the letter of the activity which provides direct practice for the objective.

12.

Objective: The child will be able to formulate appropriate spelling rules when given a number of words which exemplify a given rule.

Activity A: The child is given a list of spelling rules and words, and practices matching words to appropriate rules.

Activity B: The child is given four words in the consonant-vowel-consonant pattern and asked to tell what the words have in common.

Activity C: The child practices spelling each of his reading words.

The correct answer is activity *B*.

Now by Number 13, in your own words, write out rules one and two.

If necessary, check back in the text to see if you have stated the rules properly.

The startling generalization which should occur to you is that teaching reading by employing a systematic method will involve the identification of many explicit subobjectives which you can state. Further, in the teaching of reading, the actual arranging of activities for your students will tend to change. You will probably have a variety of activity for your children, each taking only a limited amount of time but each relevant to a particular subskill in the task of reading. Such a procedure may, at the outset, tax your patience. But a highly structured, yet variable routine can work in your classroom.

In addition, what you will be doing will have the unqualified support of many experts in the field of instruction. Instructional psychologists state that unless the particular subtasks of a complex skill are isolated and opportunity to practice is provided, there is little chance that many children will learn to read with more proficiency than at present. The second major reason (beside the planning of instruction) for teaching children to read under the guidance of objectives is the basis for evaluation such objectives provide. Very rarely do teachers of reading devise tests which adequately measure clear objectives because of the great success of standardized testing programs across the nation. Naturally, teachers feel that their own testing is a superfluous venture, since the scores on the *PZR* or some other esoteric, commercially produced test will tell them how their students are doing. Teachers are led into this position by the overreliance on these tests by those who use test scores to assess the position of their school or district by comparing them with the scores of other schools or districts. Whatever the administrative problem, the danger in allowing commercially produced tests to dominate the testing field is that the teacher has only a very gross estimate of what the reading capabilities of his students are.

The difficulty is inherent in the manner in which the selected commercially prepared test was constructed.

Suppose you are a firm believer in phonics instruction. You provide extensive practice opportunities for your students in letter sounds and synthesis of words. Yet your children score well below their grade level on the reading test administered in your school. By Number 14 circle the letter of inference from the data.

14.
A.   The class was probably below average in ability.
B.   My teaching was inadequate.
C.   The test may not measure my classroom objectives.

The best answer is probably *C,* although choice *B* and even *A* are not totally unreasonable. It would be highly desirable to have a test which did take into account the distinct program of reading instruction that individual teachers are using. Commercial reading tests have to be broad enough to take into account all possible variations of emphasis in reading instruction. Teacher evaluations based on a test which focused on comprehension, or extrapolation from data, would undoubtedly be biased against a teacher who emphasized a word attack approach to primary grade reading.

Suppose your program is largely centered around your children's ability to read stories aloud and then tell in their own words what has happened in the story. Can you think of one major reason that commercially produced and group administered reading tests might not be adequate reflections of your instruction? Write your answer next to Number 15.

You should have noted that while the objective calls for individual oral responses, the tests call for written responses.

> *Rule Three:* Write test items which adequately measure your objectives.

Thus, rule three becomes important. Implementing this rule by writing test items which measure your objectives is a relatively simple task. The hard thinking comes with rule one, the original statement of instructional goals. Suppose your objective is that your students could say the sounds of the consonants when they see them in initial positions. Next to Number 16 on the answer sheet write two or three test items to measure this objective.

16.

Objective: Students will be able to say sounds of consonants in initial positions.

Your items could be something like this:

What sound does the first letter make in each of these words? cat, dog, man.

Or perhaps something like this:

What is the sound that each of these letters makes?
S_ _ _, N_ _ _, F_ _ _.

For this next objective, write a way to test your children next to Number 17.

17.
Objective: The child will be able to read aloud from his reader.

OBJECTIVE: THE CHILD WILL READ ALOUD FROM HIS READER....

If you wrote something like this, you were half-right.

Listen to each child read aloud from his reader.

The difficulty here is in the statement of the objective. Adequate criteria for judging the child's reading were not stated. So, while it would be helpful for you to listen to the children, your testing would become more objective, and likely more reliable, if you had decided on certain attributes of oral reading on which to concentrate.

For example, a record sheet could well be made for the objective below.

Objective: The child will read aloud from his reader.

Perhaps the record sheet would look like this:

Record Sheet

Name _____

Errors:

regularly spelled words	*irregularly spelled words*	*new words*
//	////-	////

Now, for review, beside Number 18 on the answer sheet write rules two and three.

You should have indicated that rule two calls for the provision of practice on all objectives, and rule three calls for the construction of tests which are congruent with the objectives.

The final rule for the teaching of reading is that frequent testing of pupils is required.

Rule Four: Test frequently.

This rule is not stated just to create work for you. If you test your students frequently with respect to objectives, you'll be in a position to evaluate the progress of your children more adequately, and therefore to make judgments about the effectiveness of your instruction.

Four rules for reading instruction:
1. Describe objective clearly.
2. Provide practice for each objective.
3. Devise tests which measure each objective.
4. Test frequently.

The use of this four-point plan will probably be very satisfying to you. You will be able to see the results you are getting and rapidly become more efficient in your teaching. You will accumulate adequate records for each child to judge his individual differences to an extent previously impossible.

Next to Number 19 list the four rules for the teaching of reading.

19.
Four rules for reading instruction:
1. _____
2. _____
3. _____
4. _____

The correct answers are:

Four rules for reading instruction:
1. Describe your objectives explictly.
2. Provide practice.
3. Use tests which measure your objectives.
4. Test frequently.

Of course, all of these rules are meant to be used in the context of your own teaching style. Your reading instruction should be a dynamic process where objectives, practice, and testing interact with each other to result in dramatic improvement in your children's reading. Overall, remember that their reading achievement depends more on you than on abstract concepts of "readiness."

Many classroom teachers unfamiliar with how to teach reading think that a reading teacher must perform a set of mysterious and exotic things to make readers out of nonreaders. But much of the mystery disappears when these novices try to isolate the really critical skills involved in reading, then follow the four rules outlined in this program. Fortunately, such objectives-bank agencies as the Instructional Objectives Exchange* now make available large collections of measurable instructional objectives in reading (and test items as well). Equipped with such objectives and a teaching strategy consonant with the rules given here, most classroom teachers can become proficient at helping their pupils learn to master the all-important skill of reading.

*Box 24095, Los Angeles, California 90024.

Opening
Classroom
Structure

Objectives

At the conclusion of the program you should be able to:

I. Describe three observable characteristics and two instructional planning recommendations associated with open structure classrooms.

2. Classify phrases which describe classroom environments more closely related to open structures.

3. Suggest specific ways you could implement the five attributes of open structure for particular classroom situations.

Educational critics have been observing the results of school-based instruction with increasing alarm. Their attention has been directed not only to familiar problems of poor achievement in important content areas such as reading, but also to more pervasive and potentially more important dimensions. These observers have raised serious questions about practices which have always been accepted without concern but which may have negative effects on personal development.

This program will focus on educational ideas designed to counteract the destructive potential of school environments. You will learn to describe observable characteristics of classroom organization which are considered to be either positive or negative factors in the development of independence. Hopefully, you will incorporate the constructive characteristics described in this program into the situation in which you teach.

In order to examine this "new" approach, we will need to clinically consider some existing patterns in many classrooms. In our descriptions we will overgeneralize a bit for the sake of contrast. Start by considering a "typical" elementary school classroom in which the children are sitting quietly, working on assignments. The teacher, after making these assignments, spends time maintaining both records and order. Who is the center of attention in most classrooms? Answer by Number 1 on your answer sheet.

The teacher is usually the most important person in any classroom. Research on the interaction of teachers and students in classroom settings has determined that, in the classrooms sampled, over 85 percent of verbal interaction was instituted by the teacher. About three-fourths of the time the teachers provided information, directions, and corrections to the stu-

dents. Thus only a relatively small percentage of classroom talk was initiated or conducted by students. In most classrooms the teacher is an authority figure, and many of the habits of organization and procedure serve to emphasize his dominant role. Student dependence is built into the classroom both subtly and blatantly, for students somehow learn, perhaps in their first kindergarten class, that they should attend to what the teacher wants, what the teacher thinks is important.

Of course, teachers are paid to be in charge; that is their job. Critics of present educational practices have worried that the emphasis on the teacher has produced a closed classroom environment, an environment bounded by what a given teacher perceives as important, and limited by what any one instructor can bring to the instructional situation. This environment may emphasize obedience to the teacher as an authority figure rather than respect for instructional competence. These critics encourage a more "open" structure for the school room in which the direction for learning can come from a variety of sources, and the primary actors are the *students*, not the teachers. Some advocates of "open" schools have lost so much faith in educational practices that they are, in effect, calling for a moratorium on teaching. Their version of "openness" seems to have as its primary activity the avoidance of any kind of systematic learning.

The viewpoint taken in this program is distinctly different. Although a profound and dramatic change in the teacher's orientation to the authority role is probably desirable, the program will focus both on characteristics of classroom organization which can be rather easily changed and on more pervasive changes in instructional planning. It is presumed that if such changes are made, substantial modifications in teacher attitudes will follow.

Let's look at specific classroom patterns designed to reinforce the teacher's status as an authority figure. In a traditionally conducted classroom desks or chairs are arranged in neat rows. Once set, the furniture is rarely moved; sometimes

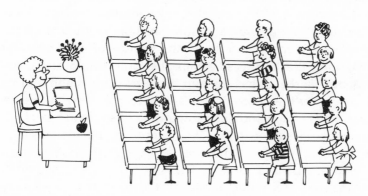

it is even nailed to the floor! How does this arrangement emphasize the teacher's authority? Briefly write your answer by Number 2.

2.
How does the usual arrangement of classroom furniture reinforce the teacher's authority status?

You might have said something like this: the desks are usually facing the teacher's desk, a podium from which the teacher speaks, or the front of the class where the teacher usually stands. Such a pattern tends to diminish the contributions of individual students. For instance, in a discussion, sometimes students can't talk to each other: they have to direct all their remarks to the teacher. The position of desks and chairs forces a constraint upon the discussion. Yet such dysfunctional furniture arrangements are accepted by teachers as immutable, and even those teachers who wish to renounce some of their vested authority are governed by the tyranny of neat rows.

The appearance of an "open" classroom displays a more flexible approach to room arrangement. Chairs and people are movable, and changes in furniture placement are directed by changes in activity. Small groups might meet in clusters of chairs or desks. The location of furniture might change from day to day, or during the class period. The teacher's desk usually does not occupy a central position. Is the importance of a flexible atmosphere worth the trouble of arranging and rearranging the furniture? Again, the logic supporting movable people and chairs is derived from the proposition that the teacher is not the central classroom figure. So it is not necessary to have chairs and desks uniformly lined up in a performer-audience relationship. The furniture position should conform to the instructional needs of the students, and these needs are expected to vary. The students do not subjugate their instructional requirements to the pattern of the chairs.

Thus, the first observable characteristic of open classrooms is an arrangement of furniture which is flexible and facilitates interaction among students.

1. Furniture arrangement:	1.	is flexible
	2.	promotes student exchange

Such arrangements contrast with those which emphasize the teacher's authority.

A second observable characteristic of an open structure classroom is the availability and arrangement of instructional materials. In a traditional classroom, all students usually work on the same set of materials at about the same time. Even in classes where children are grouped according to ability or experience, the material itself may remain identical. Answer this question by circling either true or false by Number 3 on your answer sheet.

3.
A single set of materials tends to foster independence of learning.

We would say that the answer is false. It is certainly easier for a teacher to be *in control* of instruction in the classroom when identical materials are used by every student. The authority role of the teacher is further supported by the manner in which materials or assignments are made available to students. Give your answer to the next question by Number 4 on your answer sheet.

4.
In most classrooms, instructional resources are controlled by the
A. Students
B. Teacher

Instructional resources are usually controlled by teachers rather than by students, so you should have circled *B*. Texts,

workbooks, and other instructional resources are often distributed by the teacher or a designated monitor. If special materials are needed by a particular student, he must often secure permission to get them from a locked cupboard or secret cache the teacher has assembled. It is almost as if a teacher must physically touch the materials to give them the power they need to instruct.

In an open structure classroom, materials are arranged so that students have free access to them. The teacher does not act as a middleman, as a distributor. Students can use in class those materials they need for their varied purposes, and new materials are frequently added to the collection. These materials may be obtained from the community members or brought in by the students themselves. Thus, the second observable characteristic of an open structure classroom is that instructional materials are freely accessible to the students.

    I.   Arrangement of furniture emphasizes student exchange and is flexible.

    2.   Instructional materials are various and accessible to students.

An additional point related to the availability of instructional materials relates to the autonomy with which a student may use them. Dr. Evan Keislar of the UCLA faculty has described the importance of producing *autonomous* learners. Such people don't normally depend upon the visage of authority to motivate their actions. They are able to initiate and sustain their intellectual interest without sources of external reward. Such students can pursue creative and independent lines of inquiry. How can teachers encourage the development of autonomous learning? Even in a classroom where furniture has been flexibly arranged and materials are freely accessible, one would have little reason to believe that autonomous learning would be an inevitable consequence. The very nature of the learning materials themselves must be inspected. Materials could, for example, be readily available for the student. However, if directions for their use must be secured from the teacher on an individual basis, the development of independence may be inhibited. Similarly, suppose a student is working on a set of mathematics problems. Under which conditions would you expect independence to be fostered? Answer by Number 5 on your answer sheet.

5.
A.   The student checks his answers with the teacher.
B.   The student has access to correct answers and necessary explanations without relying on the teacher.

Again, if dependence upon authority is to be reduced, we would suggest that answer *B* should have been selected, and an answer key should at least be provided for the student.

Answer by Number 6 on your answer sheet.

6.
As teacher authority decreases, student independence_____.

A word like "increases" should have been written.

The third observable attribute of open structure classroom is:

3. Students should be able to use instructional re-
    sources with a minimum of teacher assistance.

This recommendation implies that a habit will have to be broken. The teacher must stop imagining himself as the giver of all knowledge. Of course, many times a teacher will have to orient students to the proper use of instructional materials, but this activity should be done efficiently, in order to reduce unnecessary procedural dependence by the student.

Certain types of materials clearly lend themselves best to independent use. Well-designed instructional programs can

reduce the need for close supervision by the teacher, since such materials usually provide both sequenced practice and a way for the learner to measure his progress. Other appropriate materials, developed by Montessori, have been designed so that younger children can assemble sections of objects or can fit parts of a puzzle together after learning certain spatial or mathematical concepts. However, it is not necessary to secure specially designed, expensive instructional materials. The provision of simple directions and answer keys could transform traditionally available materials, such as texts and problem sheets, into those which foster independence.

By Number 7 on your answer sheet, see if you remember the three major observable requirements for open structure classrooms.

7.
Observable requirements for open structure:
1. _____
2. _____
3. _____

In any words and order you should have listed:

> *Observable requirements for open structure:*
> 1. Room arrangement is flexible and fosters student interaction.
> 2. Instructional materials are various and are directly accessible to the students.
> 3. Instructional resources can be used by students with a minimum of dependence upon the teacher.

These characteristics relate primarily to the nature and arrangement of objects and things in a classroom. Their use can be observed by entering a classroom, and the extent to which they function appropriately can be clearly evaluated.

A second area of concern for open structure classrooms relates to a less tangible category: who controls the choices of learning endeavors for the students. The notion of learner autonomy implies independence—independence not merely in authority, but also in the choice of inquiry which the students elect to pursue. In an open structure classroom, students must be given some element of choice in what they learn, in the goals of instruction. Instructional goals are formulated cooperatively by both teachers and students. These goals may be based on the learner's needs and interest as well as the content requirements of the subject area.

4. Choice of instructional goals is made jointly by students and teachers.

If a teacher teaches remedial reading, collaborative choice of goal would presuppose that some form of reading would be emphasized. Perhaps the standards for achievement, for specific performance levels, could be supplied by the students. Providing an opportunity for student involvement in the choice of objectives does not imply that anything goes—the perfection of woodcarving ability or increased competence in solving algebra problems would not be considered acceptable alternatives in the reading area, even if the students were very interested in acquiring skills in those areas.

Teachers who wish to try to use open structure are *not* giving up their instructional responsibility. Rather they are attempting to shed uncomfortable authority roles which are not essential to promoting learning and which may have negative impact on the development of independent learning by students. Suppose that cooperative planning for instructional goals were adopted in your classroom. Would you expect a curriculum to emerge which would be more uniform (A) or more diverse (B) than present practice? Answer by Number 8 on your answer sheet.

You should have marked *A,* we think. Surely the more individual student input solicited, the more likely that the goals of instruction will differ. The recommendation for implementing unstructured open classroom situations is that instructional goals should be planned cooperatively.

A coordinate precept to the collaborative selection of instructional goals is related to the actual learning process itself. It suggests that students be involved in the design of the instructional activities they will be expected to participate in. Even when those goals are shared by the group, different students may opt for varying methods to reach them. Students' learning styles vary substantially: some people learn best from well-organized print, others from discussion, and still others do best when presented with clever filmstrips embellished with gorgeous and devastatingly satirical illustrations. Unfortunately, present expertise in test development does not permit the reliable identification of students who perform best under different instructional treatments. Our suggestion is to allow students a major voice in determining the way in which they learn.

> 5.   Students should be given responsibility to develop their own learning routes.

With the teacher's guidance students should make their choices from existing instructional options. Where present resources are inadequate, plans should be made for developing more suitable instructional opportunities. Students can take primary responsibility for the development of instructional activities. Students in the primary age levels may be given choices in some areas, but not in others. Again, the teacher is not renouncing his or her role as an instructional expert, as one who is specially qualified to make certain decisions. Instead, in those areas of previously arbitrary decision greater student contribution should be permitted. When students feel that available instructional resources are inadequate, they should be encouraged to bring in outside experts or otherwise supplement the usual techniques.

By allowing student choice of instructional procedures, the open structure environment takes on one of its salient characteristics—a great variety of activity. The open classroom looks different than what most of us experienced for the twelve years we spent in school.

For the following descriptions of classrooms, classify those which you think are more likely to be associated with open classrooms than conventional organizational structures by circling the letter of each open structure description. Answer by Number 9 on your answer sheet.

9.
A. Neat and symmetrical room arrangement.
B. Variety of instructional materials.
C. Cooperative goal determination.
D. Instructional resources distributed by teacher.
E. Majority of students working on same objective.
F. Appearance of order.

We think that you should have circled letters *B* and *C*. Please note that the phrases associated with letters *A, D, E, F,* represent the common, if overgeneralized, notion of what a traditional classroom looks like. If you decide to make some changes in such orderly structures, you should be prepared for a period of adjustment—first by your students, who may assume that reduced appearance of authority means that you don't care about learning; second, by your colleagues and administrators, who may be used to symmetry and quiet in the schools. You will have to demonstrate that learning is taking place. If you can be convincing, you can perhaps interest them in experimenting with a less authority-bound classroom. Parents, too, may need reassurance; the reports they receive from their children could possibly alarm them and make any changes more difficult for you. In fact, before beginning a modified instructional pattern, you might meet with parents to orient them to your plans.

Five major points have been emphasized so far in this program. See if you can briefly describe them on your answer sheet by Number 10. The first three techniques related to observable characteristics. The second two points were recommendations regarding planning.

10.
Requirements for open structure classroom
Observable characteristics:
1. _____
2. _____
3. _____
Recommendations for instructional planning:
4. _____
5. _____

Requirements for open structure classroom
Observable characteristics:
1. Room arrangement is flexible and fosters student interaction.
2. Instructional materials are freely accessible to students.
3. Instructional materials may be used with a minimum dependence upon the teacher.

Instructional planning recommendations:
4. Instructional goals are cooperatively developed by students and teachers.
5. Students are encouraged to choose methods for learning.

For the next section of the program, you are going to be asked to identify elements of classroom organization or instructional planning which do not adhere to the basic idea of open structure. You should try to suggest specific ways of incorporating the five major points previously described. There will be, however, no single right answer for any one exercise. The purpose of this section is to encourage your thinking of ways to change present practices.

Here's an easy one. Your class wishes to have an extended discussion series on the democratic process. But your classroom looks like this:

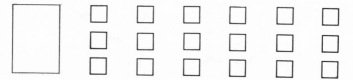

Answer by Number 11 on your answer sheet. You may either sketch or write your answer.

Arrangements such as these would have been satisfactory, or you might have said "Move the desks around." For the next

desks in background

people on floor

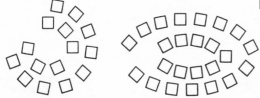

exercise, suppose you are in the same situation as before, but the desks and chairs are permanently attached to the floor. Briefly describe what you might do by Number 12 on your answer sheet.

If you are a firebrand, you might have suggested a crowbar and explosives to change the seating arrangement but that is one of the few *wrong* answers. More feasible would be moving the people around. They might perch on desks—or meet outside, or sit on the floor or on stage in the auditorium.

Try this next situation. Having a thrifty background, you tend to keep dictionaries, texts, and workbooks securely locked in the closet. How can you productively change the situation? Answer by Number 13 on your answer sheet.

We do not recommend giving each student a key to the closet. Pillage and/or plunder are likely to follow. Instead you might have your materials arranged on tables according to topics or tasks. A superb open response might have included involving all or at least part of student decision-making in your choice.

Here's another exercise:

Suppose your instructional materials consisted of conventional classroom resources such as textbooks, exercises, dictionaries, or other reference works. What could you do to facilitate the independent use of the materials? Write your response by Number 14 on your answer sheet.

One simple thing would be to prepare written or taped directions to assist the students with materials whose uses were not clear.

Second, you could have suggested that you would prepare answer keys for any problem set or exercises. If you were feeling extra ambitious, you could also provide directions so that pairs or small groups of students might initiate structured discussions without depending on you. At first such directions need to be fairly specific but as students become accustomed to being responsible for their own learning, less detail will probably be required for success.

In this next hypothetical situation, suppose you were embarking on a new topic. Imagine that you wished to treat some broad historical concept. How would you incorporate the recommendations for instructional planning into your deliberations? List specific ways you might do so by Number 15 on your answer sheet.

If you were committed to obtaining student input in the selection of instructional goals, you might have done some of the following things.

1. Had a discussion to delimit the general area of concern for the students.
2. Asked student groups to identify alternative tasks and report back.

3. Permit individual students to negotiate their personal instructional objectives in a conference with you.

To encourage independent choice and pursuit of learning opportunity students might have:

1. Had individual conferences with the teacher to decide on what their immediate plans would be.
2. Within a limited time period searched for and evaluated available instructional materials.
3. Surveyed your colleagues for information related to the instruction, and provided the students with a broad choice of activities.

To restate, if as a teacher you are concerned with the development of independence in learning, experiment with the recommendations in this program. Remember that not only are your habits going to undergo a change, but also so are the expectations of your students, colleagues, and community members. To begin, you might limit your first attempts at a more open approach to a particular area of instruction or to only one class. To encourage student independence, you will have to provide an "experimental" environment. The requirements of open structure described here represent the barest outline of what is necessary. Try it and see if it works.

Requirements for open structure classroom
Observable characteristics:
1. Room arrangement is flexible and fosters student interaction.
2. Instructional materials are freely accessible to students.
3. Instructional materials may be used with a minimum dependence upon the teacher.

Instructional planning recommendations:
4. Instructional goals are cooperatively developed by students and teachers.
5. Students are encouraged to choose preferred methods for learning.

Discipline
in the
Classroom

Objectives

For most beginning teachers (and for many experienced ones, too) the problems associated with maintaining proper classroom control loom significant. Research on classroom discipline problems yields less than satisfying results. The study of disciplinary tactics and situations in which to use them represents one of the most un-researched areas in the field of education.

But practicing classroom teachers cannot wait for definitive research results to maintain proper classroom control; their problem is immediate. Accordingly, this program attempts to provide some guidance for classroom teachers faced with disciplinary dilemmas.

Specifically, at the conclusion of the program the reader will be able to:

1. List the six disciplinary rules given in the program.
2. Identify whether teachers' responses to hypothetical disciplinary situations are consistent with those six rules.
3. Given the description of a discipline problem, to propose in writing a solution which is in accord with the principles stated in the program.

When prospective teachers are asked to name their Number One Problem, what do you think they usually say? Circle the letter of the correct response by Number 1 on the answer sheet.

1.
A. Bringing about learning
B. Inadequate materials
C. Class size
D. Discipline

If you marked discipline, you are correct. Many practicing teachers and prospective teachers are extremely concerned about discipline, or classroom management. The assertion that an exciting learning program is the best preventative of classroom problems does little to assuage their anxieties.

Teachers are unsure of the best way to proceed, particularly when they are confronting students with values different from their own, and worry that the class will get out of hand.

To most teachers discipline seems to mean that precious control of the classroom. Control, of course, does not always imply strictness; it does imply authority at the level at which each individual teacher feels comfortable. Would you think that teachers would all choose about the same degree of classroom control? Answer Yes or No by Number 2.

Obviously, a negative answer would be the better choice. Since individual differences are prominent among teachers as well as students, the relative strictness or leniency will vary greatly. Flexibility, satisfaction with the instructional responsibilities, and so on, would be highly influential in the degree of control any particular teacher wished to exert. It would be both a senseless and hopeless enterprise, then, to describe specific actions which should inevitably be undertaken in all classrooms. Because the teacher's personality, the setting, the student population, the age level, and the subject matter vary, there is little empirical evidence that any given action is always successful. Further, there is a lack of data indicating any relationship between the students' accomplishment of different objectives and the type of discipline imposed on the class.

Then what do you do? With the dramatic void of research, why not abstain from any systematic consideration of the area, run a "tight ship," and hope for the best?

There is at least one important reason we should not leave discipline to chance: psychologists and educators most concerned with instruction have repeatedly pointed out that learning and attitude are closely related. And we wish to promote reasonable attitudes in students. Repressive techniques in the management of the class are not likely to aid in positive attitude development.

There is, however, a highly rational way to approach classroom control. The system has been demonstrated in disparate situations, with elementary school pupils as well as delinquent youths. Basically, there are a number of simple rules, extrapolated from reinforcement literature in the psychology of learning, through which behavior changes are accomplished by rewards.

The first rule states a precondition for effective control: the teacher should attend to observable student behavior. Mrs. Jones punished an entire classful of students for the misbehavior of little Joey, who stuck out his tongue in an unusually repulsive fashion. She took action which affected the entire class rather than just the particular student. Perhaps Mrs. Jones was in a peculiarly bad mood. But if she had attended to and evaluated the seriousness and pervasiveness of the misbehavior, it would be unlikely that she would have responded the way she did.

Try to write in your own words, the first rule for classroom discipline. Answer by Number 3 on the answer sheet.

You should have written something like the following:

Rule One: Attend to observable behavior.

Is a teacher adhering to rule one if he senses that the students are about to create trouble and therefore makes a punitive reading assignment? Answer Yes or No by Number 4.

Unless the teacher "sensed trouble" because he observed some students *actually* breaking rules, the answer should be no. Rule one is obviously insufficient to solve any classroom behavior problem; standards to judge the propriety of students' actions are also needed. The teacher should precisely delineate in his mind likely unacceptable student behaviors. Such forethought, while not exhausting all the scintillating ways students might misbehave, enable a teacher to plan responses to probable categories of misconduct in advance. He is less likely to be caught unaware and to make a response to a student that both will regret. Different teachers will, of course, have different prohibitions. A strict teacher might have a long list of restrictions, while a lenient teacher might have a short one. Both teachers would profit from some forethought on the problem of classroom control.

Not only is it important for the teacher to formulate these rules of acceptable behavior, but in some manner he should communicate to the students what is expected of them in the way of deportment. Such information ought not to be tossed, gauntlet-like, to the class, inviting tests of will and restraint. Yet for a teacher to secretly harbor a set of verboten behaviors and delight in "catching" the students in his trap is surely a misuse of energy and very likely an exercise in sadism.

Rule Two: Define limits of acceptable behavior and communicate these to your class.

Is the following teacher using rule two? Answer Yes or No next to Number 5 on the answer sheet.

5.
Sally brings her transistor radio to class. Using the ear phone attachment, she listens to the radio after completing her assignment. Mrs. Gordon approaches her and says she is sorry but radios are not allowed in her classroom. Toward the end of the period she jokes about Sally's ingenuity and restates that radios will not be permitted.

Of course the answer is Yes. The teacher not only told the offender but communicated the rule to the other members of the class. Now see if you can recall the first two rules we have discussed. Using your own words write both of these rules by Number 6 on the answer sheet.

6.
Rule One _____

Rule Two _____

The first two rules are as follows:

> *Rule One:* Attend to observable behavior.
> *Rule Two:* Define limits of acceptable behavior and communicate these to your class.

These two rules merely set the conditions under which a teacher can respond to classroom management problems. Without them, he will likely respond more often than necessary to episodes, both real and imagined, of classroom disturbance. The next three closely linked discipline rules are drawn directly from the writings of psychologists involved in the study of human behavior. The underlying idea is that if you want a behavior to recur, reward it. If you want a behavior to disappear, ignore it, and reward an alternate response.

> *Rule Three:* Do not reward undesired behavior.

Let us examine this rule. We have already focused on and defined undesired behaviors in rules one and two. When a student is engaged in action contrary to stated limits, do not reward him. While sounding obvious, the rule is often violated.

For the following exercise try to determine if the fictitious teacher is using rule three. Answer Yes or No by Number 7.

7.

Mrs. Blotch is trying to get through a difficult algebra lesson. Her students are being abnormally disruptive. In distress, she stops the lesson and allows the students to work on their homework.

You should have answered no. Mrs. Blotch actually rewarded misbehavior by allowing the students class time to do their homework.

In this next example attempt to decide if the teacher is adhering to rule three. Answer Yes or No by Number 8.

8.

Scott is a demanding eight-year-old boy who likes the teacher's attention. He begins to pound on his desk. Mr. Smith pretends that he is not aware of what he is doing.

The answer should be Yes. Providing attention, even scolding, could be interpreted as a reward to a demanding child. It would be better to ignore disruptive behavior when it will not seriously interfere with other children's well-being.

See, if in the space beside Number 9, you can write the three rules we have discussed so far.

9.

Rule One _____

Rule Two _____

Rule Three _____

You should have written something like the following:

> *Rule One:* Attend to observable behavior.
> *Rule Two:* Define limits of acceptable behavior and communicate these to your class.
> *Rule Three:* Do not reward undesired behavior.

Can we expect unrewarded behavior to disappear? Is it reasonable to assume that a child will simply stop misbehaving when his misbehavior goes unnoticed? There is some evidence that behavior which goes unrewarded does tend to disappear. If the first time a baby says "Mama," he is not greeted with squeals of delight, hugs, and kisses, it is not likely that he will repeat the word very soon. Unfortunately, the teacher cannot always wait patiently until the problem student stops disturbing the class. In a classroom situation, what then should be done with the rule violator? Should he

be punished? Teachers have often decided to make the disruptive student stay after school, go to the principal's office, or perhaps be spanked. In general, punishment seems to have little effect in inhibiting behavior. And there is some logic in the argument that punishment, as doled out in the schools, often means more school work for the student. It does not take long for a student to build up bad associations for homework when he sees that the teacher assigns more of it in response to classroom disorder.

Rule Four: Avoid punishing undesired behaviors.

Avoiding repressive punishment would certainly modify the attitude of students toward the teacher's role in school. When a child is punished, anxiety occurs not only in the offender but in other students as well. Punishment also gets the teacher into other difficulty. When a teacher habitually punishes misbehavior, he may develop a tendency to use the *threat* of punishment as a weapon in the classroom.

"If you throw paper one more time I shall make you stand in the corner."

The teacher's threat may have been made in anger. Unless he now follows through when more paper is thrown, all further threats will be ineffective. Further, the teacher may be committed to this punishment in all future cases of this type. When the problem is compounded by the lack of evidence that punishment is successful in changing behavior, there seems little reason to involve oneself in a potential source of additional classroom difficulty.

Is the teacher in this next example adhering to rule four? Examine the exercise, then circle Yes or No next to Number 10.

10.
Emily and Janet are best friends and like to spend most of their classroom time in their junior high school talking to each other. Their behavior is very annoying to their English teacher. In an effort to put a stop to this demeanor once and for all, the teacher warns

the girls that if they talk they will have to stay after school. When the girls do talk, they are required to remain after school until 4:00. The teacher is satisfied that he has been consistent. Is he adhering to rule four?

The answer should be No. The English teacher may be satisfied that he was consistent. Unfortunately, he has no basis for deciding that this consistency will at all modify the girls' tendency to talk.

See if by Number 11 you can list the four rules of classroom control described so far.

11.
Rule One _____
Rule Two _____
Rule Three _____
Rule Four _____

Your answer should have looked something like this.

> *Rule One:* Attend to observable behavior.
> *Rule Two:* Define limits of acceptable behavior and communicate these to your class.
> *Rule Three:* Do not reward undesired behaviors.
> *Rule Four:* Avoid punishing undesired behaviors.

So far, you have been told what *not* to do when confronted with behavior problems in the classroom. You should not reward—even inadvertently—undesired responses. And, generally, you should not punish or threaten to punish student misbehavior. While there is research and theoretical support for ignoring misbehavior, the practical considerations of the classroom may make this a relatively trying alternative.

Rule five provides some guidance about what you can actually do to solve some of your chronic problems.

> *Rule Five:* Provide an acceptable alternative student response for undesired behavior.

Suppose, for example, a child in your class begins to read comic books instead of the text. To send him to the principal would violate one of the earlier rules. But suppose, instead, you provide him with a book to read other than the text, saying, "Comic books are not allowed, but *here is* a book which might interest you." Or if your students complain about the amount of homework assigned, allow them to decide together with you what an equitable amount of work would be. Essentially, in both cases, you are channeling the students' behavior into an appropriate area.

Is the teacher in this next example adhering to rule five? Answer Yes or No by Number 12.

12.
Mark brings a doughnut into class following the mid-morning break. Mr. Brown says, "Mark, put that doughnut away. You know I don't allow food in this class."

While Mr. Brown was employing rules one and two (he actually observed misbehavior and communicated the limits again to Mark), he did not provide an acceptable alternate response for Mark to make. You should have circled the no. The teacher might have said something like, "Put the doughnut away; food is not permitted in this class. Why don't you go get a drink of water?" The drink may not have been as satisfying, but would have provided something for the reprimanded student to do.

Try another example. Is the following teacher using rule five? Answer Yes or No by Number 13.

13.
Jerry always waves his hand and shouts out when he knows the right answer. The teacher calls Jerry to his desk and says that this behavior is not in order. He suggests that Jerry may, if he wishes, write an extra assignment, summarizing some of the major points in the reading.

The answer should be Yes, for the teacher has allowed Jerry a way to express himself in an approved fashion.

The final guideline, rule six, is very simple.

Rule Six: Reward appropriate behaviors.

When a student has substituted an appropriate behavior for a previously undesired response, do not let this change go unnoticed. Reward the student. Use praise or provide the opportunity to engage in a desired activity, such as going to the library or taking roll for the class. The same reasoning holds true for desired as well as undesired responses: if they are ignored, they will tend to disappear. Sometimes teachers become so involved with misdeeds that they don't properly acknowledge appropriate behavior. Thus, "good" responses may extinguish.

A second problem exists in trying to ascertain what an appropriate reward or "reinforcer" for the student might be. Opportunity to read books in the library might be a reward for some students but a punishment to others. Similarly, a chance to run an errand might be highly desirable to particular students, but viewed as banishment or extra work by others. The

"GEORGIE, PLEASE RUN AND DELIVER THIS NOTE....TO BOLIVIA!"

teacher can judge the appropriateness of rewards only when he thinks he understands what kind of people his students are. For example, seeing an educational closed circuit TV program might be rewarding to students who do not have television at home. But for children who have color television sets, the prospect of watching a black and white program may not be as enthralling. For some children, playing competitive games is an exciting experience. Other children may find competition threatening and seek to avoid it. So while this rule is simple, it has many complicating aspects.

One other point should be made. If a child has been practicing inappropriate responses, don't wait for a complete reversal before rewarding him; praise each step he makes toward desired responses. If Matthew rarely comes to class, don't wait until he has perfect attendance for a week to reward him. Reward him the first time he comes into the classroom. You can begin to shape his behavior in the desired direction.

For this next example, determine if the teacher is using rule six in dealing with classroom behavior problems. Answer Yes or No by Number 14.

14.

John is usually tardy to class. Friday he comes in on time. Miss Paul takes roll, and when John responds, she comments sarcastically that she can't take the shock. Is Miss Paul using rule six?

The answer is No. She not only does not reward John's behavior, she punishes him by mocking him.

If you can, recall all six rules of discipline in the classroom. Answer by Number 15 on your answer sheet.

15.

Rule One _____

Rule Two _____

Rule Three _____

Rule Four _____

Rule Five _____

Rule Six _____

Did you remember them all?

> *Rule One:* Attend to observable behavior.
> *Rule Two:* Define limits of acceptable behavior and communicate these to your class.
> *Rule Three:* Do not reward undesired behaviors.
> *Rule Four:* Avoid punishing undesired behaviors.
> *Rule Five:* Provide an acceptable alternative student response for undesired behavior.
> *Rule Six:* Reward appropriate behaviors.

Let's see if you can determine whether the following teachers are adhering to the approach advocated through these rules.

Is Mrs. Lane adhering to the principles discussed in the program? Answer Yes or No by Number 16.

16.
Bob and Patty are passing notes in their English class. Mrs. Lane first warns them, then intercepts a note and reads it to the class.

Your answer should be No. Mrs. Lane responds to the problem by embarrassing the students.

Answer this next example by Number 17.

17.
Rita cries in school. Mrs. Gates hugs her whenever she cries to try and make her feel better.

Again the answer should be No. Mrs. Gates is actually rewarding undesired behavior. She is not providing an alternate response for the child.

Here is another practice exercise. Answer Yes or No by Number 18.

18.
Jim does not usually do book reports. The first time he turns one in, his teacher returns it with an "F."

Again the answer should be No. The teacher is punishing Jim's response. It is not likely that many more book reports will be forthcoming from Jim.

Now see if you can actually apply the principles discussed to common classroom problems. Think through a course of action to deal with the following problem. Try to make your plan consistent with the rules presented earlier.

19.
Seven-year-old Danny promptly does his homework, but it is always messy.
Mentally plan a course of action to help with this problem.

Your solution should not include punishment or threats. The teacher should tell Danny that sloppy work is not acceptable. The teacher could point out that he might wish to make scribble drawings during art time. If he does so, he should be praised. Furthermore, any sign of neatness in homework should be complimented.

The application of these rules, just as any other instructional tactics, should result in classroom procedures which are testable against a criterion of what happens to the learner. Thus, sometimes such rule-derived plans will not succeed in bringing about the desired pupil behavior—or eliminating the undesirable pupil behavior. But when the teacher assembles his plans from a set of research-based rules rather than relying on spur-of-the-moment decisions, his resulting classroom actions should be more defensible.

Program
Answer
Sheets

Written Plans for Classroom Instruction *Answer Sheet*

1. _____

2. _____

3. _____

4. _____

5. A _____

   B _____

6. A   B   C

7. A   B   C

8. A   B   C

9. (1) _____

   (2) _____

   (3) _____

   (4) _____

   (5) _____

   (6) _____

   (7) _____

10. (1) _____

    (2) _____

    (3) _____

    (4) _____

    (5) _____

11. TU   LP   B   N

12. TU   LP   B   N

13. TU   LP   B   N

14. TU   LP   B   N

Individualizing Instruction *Answer Sheet*

1. N E M B
2. N E M B
3. N E M B
4. N E M B
5. (1) _____
   (2) _____
   (3) _____
6. Yes   No
7. (1) _____
   (2) _____
   (3) _____
   (4) _____
8. (1) _____
   (2) _____
   (3) _____
   (4) _____
9. (1) _____
   (2) _____
   (3) _____
   (4) _____

Instructional Tactics for Affective Goals *Answer Sheet*

1. Yes   No
2. A   B
3. Yes   No
4. Yes   No
5. Yes   No
6. Yes   No
7. Yes   No
8. R+   R-
9. R+   R-
10. M   C   R
11. M   C   R
12. M   C   R
13. M   C   R   N
14. M   C   R   N
15. M   C   R   N

The Teaching of Reading *Answer Sheet*

  1. A   B

  2. A   B   C

  3. Yes   No

  4. A   B   C

  5. A   B   C

  6 Rule One _____

  7. Yes   No

  8. Yes   No

  9. A   B

10. A   B

11. A   B

12. A   B   C

13. Rule One _____

     Rule Two _____

14. A   B   C

15. _____

    _____

16. _____

    _____

    _____

    _____

17. _____

    _____

18. Rule Two _____

     Rule Three _____

19. Rule One _____

     Rule Two _____

     Rule Three _____

     Rule Four _____

Opening Classroom Structure *Answer Sheet*

1. _____
2. _____
3. True   False
4. A   B
5. A   B
6. _____
7. 1. _____
   2. _____
   3. _____
8. A   B
9. A · B   C   D   E   F
10. 1. _____
    2. _____
    3. _____
    4. _____
    5. _____
11. _____
    _____
12. _____
13. _____
14. _____
15. _____
    _____

Discipline in the Classroom *Answer Sheet*

1. A   B   C   D
2. Yes   No
3. Rule One _____
4. Yes   No
5. Yes   No
6. Rule One _____
    Rule Two _____
7. Yes   No
8. Yes   No
9. Rule One _____
    Rule Two _____
    Rule Three _____
10. Yes   No
11. Rule One _____
    Rule Two _____
    Rule Three _____
    Rule Four _____
12. Yes   No
13. Yes   No
14. Yes   No
15. Rule One _____
    Rule Two _____
    Rule Three _____
    Rule Four _____
    Rule Five _____
    Rule Six _____
16. Yes   No
17. Yes   No
18. Yes   No

Mastery
Tests

Mastery Test: Written Plans for Classroom Instruction

Name _____

Part I. *Directions:* Circle the letter of the expression which is most accurately defined in each of the following four items.

_____ 1. This is a collection of possible instructional activities and references from which a teacher can plan a segment of instruction for longer than one classroom period.
   a. lesson plan   c. course of study
   b. teaching unit   d. resource unit

_____ 2. This is a description of the content and, sometimes, the objectives to be covered for a given subject matter at a given grade level.
   a. lesson plan   c. course of study
   b. teaching unit   d. resource unit

_____ 3. This is a particular plan of instruction developed by one or more teachers for a period of instruction in excess of one class period.
   a. lesson plan   c. course of study
   b. teaching unit   d. resource unit

_____ 4. This is a fairly detailed description of an instructional plan for a single class period.
   a. lesson plan   c. course of study
   b. teaching unit   d. resource unit

Part II. *Directions:* In the spaces below list *in order* seven elements which are recommended for inclusion in a teaching unit.

1. _____
2. _____
3. _____
4. _____
5. _____
6. _____
7. _____

Part III. *Directions:* In the spaces below list *in order* five elements which are recommended for inclusion in a lesson plan.

140

1. _____
2. _____
3. _____
4. _____
5. _____

Part IV. *Directions:* In each of the following questions an operation will be described. Indicate by circling the letter of the correct answer whether the operation should be carried out in the preparation of teaching units, lesson plans, both, or neither.

_____ 1. A posttest is always included.
    a. teaching units   c. both
    b. lesson plans   d. neither

_____ 2. An assignment, if there is one, is listed.
    a. teaching units   c. both
    b. lesson plans   d. neither

_____ 3. Day-by-day plans are made.
    a. teaching units   c. both
    b. lesson plans   d. neither

_____ 4. Broad, general objectives are often used here for organizational purposes.
    a. teaching units   c. both
    b. lesson plans   d. neither

_____ 5. The teacher focuses on the question: "What do I want the learners to become?"
    a. teaching units   c. both
    b. lesson plans   d. neither

_____ 6. Instructional resources are listed.
    a. teaching units   c. both
    b. lesson plans   d. neither

_____ 7. The teacher focuses on the question: "What should I do?"
    a. teaching units   c. both
    b. lesson plans   d. neither

_____ 8. Behavioral objectives are employed.
    a. teaching units   c. both
    b. lesson plans   d. neither

_____ 9. The instructional planner consults other sources to determine if curricular restrictions are present.
a. teaching units   c. both
b. lesson plans   d. neither

_____ 10. A pretest is included.
a. teaching units   c. both
b. lesson plans   d. neither

_____ 11. Criterion check is a required element.
a. teaching units   c. both
b. lesson plans   d. neither

_____ 12. A back-up lesson is recommended.
a. teaching units   c. both
b. lesson plans   d. neither

_____ 13. Teacher and learner activities are detailed with time estimates provided in minutes.
a. teaching units   c. both
b. lesson plans   d. neither

Mastery Test: Individualizing Instruction

Name _____

1. For each of the following descriptions, indicate by writing the appropriate letter whether the situation reflects no individualization *(N)*, individualized ends *(E)*, individualized means *(M)*, both individualized ends and means *(B)*.

_____ (1) Mrs. Higgins allows her fourth-grade students to pursue different topics during their reading period. She urges them to select books consonant with their abilities.

_____ (2) This geometry class moves sequentially through the major theorems of the field. The instructor believes that all students must acquire each en route skill before mastering terminal course goals.

_____ (3) Students are given several options to achieve ten specific course goals. They are allowed to use a self-study series of programmed texts, standard textbook, or frequent correlation with a small discussion-study group.

_____ (4) Mr. Poe's U.S. History class spends most of its time viewing very sophisticated films depicting important American historical events. Frequent opportunities are provided during the films for the students to respond to thought-provoking questions. After a reasonable pause, the film's narrator supplies the correct answer or, as is usually the case, alternative correct answers.

_____ (5) This continuous progress school identifies a series of specific objectives for each child on the basis of diagnostic tests, then prescribes a tailored instructional sequence deemed most appropriate for a given learner.

2. Name and briefly describe three school organization patterns recommended for individualizing instruction.

(1) _____

_____

_____

(2) _____

_____

(3) _____

_____

3. Supply the names of three or more specific instructional procedures suggested for use with *each* of the following instructional approaches.

   (1) Large group instruction:

   _____

   _____

   _____

   (2) Small group instruction:

   _____

   _____

   _____

   (3) Independent study:

   _____

   _____

   _____

Mastery Test: Instructional Tactics for Affective Goals

Name _____

Part I. In the spaces provided, briefly describe the general nature of the indicated phrases.

1. Modeling Tactics

2. Contiguity Tactics

3. Reinforcement Tactics

Part II. For each of the following fictitious accounts of educators in action, indicate whether one *or more* of the following instructional tactics are clearly being employed: *Modeling* (Circle *M*), *Contiguity* (Circle *C*), or *Reinforcement* (Circle *R*). If *None* are clearly being used, circle *N*. Thus, for example, for a given item you might circle *M* and *R*, or only *M*, or perhaps *M, C,* and *R*. Any single letter or combination of the *M, C,* or *R* tactics is possible. If you circled an *N*, of course, no other letter would appear.

M C R N 1. Mrs. Jenkins wishes to increase her pupils' positive affect for literature as reflected by their increased volitional checking out of books from the school library. She consults the school librarian's records to verify the frequency of such behavior. In an effort to achieve this goal, Mrs. Jenkins makes certain that the library's reading facilities are particularly comfortable (lounge chairs), attractive (well-decorated), and well-ventilated (adequate air circulation).

M C R N 2. A government teacher tries to foster a spirit of "world citizenship" in her students rather than highly parochial nationalistic attitudes. The teacher tries to "practice what she preaches" by engaging in verbal behavior which enthusiastically conveys her belief that we are members of a human community which crosses national boundaries. Whenever students voice a similar position, she commends them.

M C R N 3. This teacher has an affective objective that the students will learn to be diligent workers as reflected by their ability to persevere at a given assignment until its completion. Accordingly, frequent in-class and homework assignments are given to the youngsters so that they have ample opportunity to engage in this behavior.

M C R N 4. Mr. Smith wants more of the students in his inner-city high school to aspire to higher education after graduation. At least once a month he invites back former students of that school who have gone on to college and have embarked on professional careers. These former students discuss their current activities with the high school youngsters and answer questions regarding their roles, previous education, etc. Mr. Smith tries to make these occasions very positive for the students by furnishing refreshments and decorating the room especially well.

M C R N 5. A teacher in a New Mexico junior high school discovers that the air conditioning in her classroom is defective and that it is unbearably hot. Shortly after the class discussion gets underway of the previous night's reading assignment —at a point where student interest is keen— she says "Let's leave this hothouse for a while and sit on the lawn under a tree."

Mastery Test: The Teaching of Reading

Name _____

Part I. *Directions:* List four basic rules you should use in planning reading instruction.

1. _____

2. _____

3. _____

4. _____

Part II. *Directions:* Mark *X* by the following objectives which represent suitable statements of reading goals.

_____ 5. The child learns to comprehend the meaning of what he has read.

_____ 6. The child learns to attack words into their phonetic elements.

_____ 7. The child is able to say the sound of medial vowel in a simple spelling pattern.

_____ 8. The child can understand what he is reading.

_____ 9. The child is able to tell a story he reads silently so that it ends differently.

Part III. *Directions:* Which of the following is an appropriate activity for the stated objective? Circle the letter of the correct answer.

10. *Objective:* to be able to read irregular spelling words by sight
   a. to read and tell about a story in the primer
   b. to practice sounding out words into their phonetic elements
   c. to practice saying the words when presented with flashcards

11. *Objective:* to be able to sound out new words spelled regularly
   a. to practice listening to words which rhyme
   b. to be able to pronounce the consonant or consonant blend in the initial position
   c. to be able to say letter names of all consonants

Part IV. *Directions:* Write two test items to measure each of the following objectives:

> *Objective:* The child will be able to pronounce a regularly spelled word he has never seen before, using a phonetic approach.

12. Item _____

13. Item _____

> *Objective:* The child will be able to indicate that he comprehends a word by explaining its meaning orally or demonstrating its meaning.

14. Item _____

15. Item _____

Mastery Test: Opening Classroom Structure

Name _____

1. List the five attributes of open structure discussed in the program.
   a. _____
   b. _____
   c. _____
   d. _____
   e. _____

2. Circle the letter of those descriptions of classrooms which are more related to open structure than to conventional classrooms.
   a. Teacher does not "teach" from any one place.
   b. Teacher requires students to sign out for atlases.
   c. Students organize a symposium on the topic of the draft.
   d. Class looks chaotic to district supervisor.
   e. Teacher places desk where she can check up on trouble makers.
   f. Grades are determined by performance on objectives shared by the whole class.
   g. Students seem to do most of the talking.
   h. Most questions come from the teacher.
   i. Planning and coordinating instructional activities is relatively more time consuming.

3. Suppose you were presented with the following instructional problems. How would you apply open structure recommendations to help you solve them? Briefly write your answer. Be specific.
   a. Your class seems to hate history, but you strongly feel that certain historical concepts are important.

   b. Your class has 36 desks and 42 students. You would like to have an extended discussion period on aesthetics.

c. Your elementary school children annoy you by interrupting your work with a reading group with requests for direction and assistance in mathematics.

d. All students think your science class is irrelevant.

Mastery Test: Discipline in the Classroom

Name _____

Part I.

1. Suppose Karen always combed her hair in class. Consistent with the principles advocated in the program, write out a course of action you might use.

Part II. *Directions:* Are the following teachers being consistent with the point of view advocated in the program? Write "yes" or "no" in the space provided.

_____ 2. Robert is carving his initials on the face of his desk. His teacher warns him once, then sends him to the principal's office.

_____ 3. The students in Mrs. Knight's class are usually so anxious to go to lunch that the last five minutes of the period are worthless instructionally. Mrs. Knight lets her students talk quietly during this time.

_____ 4. When Joey shows up at his physical education class not wearing a regulation gym shirt, Coach Fizz sends him on a three-lap run around the track.

_____ 5. Sandy normally does not contribute to class discussion. The first time she does, her comment is irrelevant. Mr. Davies does not correct her.

_____ 6. Miss Madison overhears two students using profanity in the hall. She confronts them and tells them she will report them to their homeroom teacher, which she does.

_____ 7. Robin tends to fall on the playground. Mrs. Lopez is not very sympathetic and does not give him special attention.

Part III. List the six rules described for use in classroom discipline.

8. Rule One _____
9. Rule Two _____

152

10. Rule Three _____

11. Rule Four _____

12. Rule Five _____

13. Rule Six _____

Answers to
Mastery
Tests

Written Plans for Classroom Instruction

Part I.
1. d, 2. c, 3. b, 4. a.

Part II.
1. Precise instructional objectives
2. Pretest
3. Day-by-day activities
4. Criterion check
5. Posttest
6. Resources
7. Back-up lesson

Part III.
1. Precise instructional objectives
2. Learner activities
3. Teacher activities
4. Time estimates
5. Assignments—if any

Part IV.
1. a, 2. b, 3. a, 4. a, 5. c, 6. a, 7. d, 8. c, 9. a, 10. a, 11. a, 12. a, 13. a.

Individualizing Instruction

1. (1) E, (2) N, (3) N, (4) N, (5) B.
2. (1) Team teaching, plus reasonable description
   (2) Nongraded programs, plus reasonable description
   (3) Flexible scheduling, plus reasonable description
3. (1) Teacher lectures
      Guest speakers
      Group-paced media presentations
      Elaborate demonstrations
   (2) Discussions
      Cooperation projects
      Laboratory activities
      Subgroup presentations
   (3) Commercially prepared self-instruction materials
      Teacher developed self-instruction materials
      Instructional resource centers
      Tutorial programs

Instructional Tactics for Affective Goals

Part I.
1. Providing persons who engage in behavior the learner can imitate.
2. Arranging positive and aversive conditions so that they will be associated by the learner with the affective behavior sought.
3. Introducing positive stimuli or removing aversive stimuli after the learner engages in a desired behavior.

Part II.
1. C, 2. M, S, 3. N, 4. M, C, 5. R.

The Teaching of Reading

Part I.
1. Describe objectives clearly
2. Provide practice for each objective
3. Devise tests which measure each objective
4. Test frequently

Part II.
An *X* should be placed only before 7 and 9.

Part III.
10. c, 11. b.

Part IV.
12. Say this new word: (printed stimulus) *home*
13. Say this new word: (printed stimulus) *rag*
14. Tell me or show me what this word means: *smile*
15. Tell me or show me what this word means: *jump*

Opening Classroom Structure

1. a. Room arrangement is flexible and encourages student interaction.
   b. Instructional materials are freely accessible to students.

    c. Instructional materials can be used with minimum dependence upon the teacher.

    d. Instructional goals are cooperatively developed by students and teachers.

    e. Students are encouraged to choose preferred methods for learning.

2. You should have circled c, d, g, i.

3. a. You should provide an opportunity for your students to determine how they would like to learn the objectives associated with the historical concepts. Providing the students with knowledge about existing instructional options, or encouraging them to develop their own would apply a major point related to open structure.

    b. Move the students around. Sit on the floor or on the desks. Go outside or to the cafeteria.

    c. Try to develop a set of instructional materials which the students can get to without your help and can work through successfully with only minimal assistance from you. You might consider using puzzles made of construction paper, answer sheets for problem or work sheets, or brief introductory cassette taped directions.

    d. You have big problems. However, an appropriate answer would have involved students in formulating objectives for the class which they perceived to be relevant to their interests and which also satisfied your perception of the discipline of science. A next elaboration would have suggested the joint generation of learning activities.

Discipline in the Classroom

Part I.

1. The answer should include the following:

The teacher should tell Karen about the rule against haircombing.

The teacher should not threaten or punish Karen.

The teacher should suggest an alternate activity for Karen to engage in.

The teacher should reward Karen for engaging in the acceptable alternate behavior.

Part II.

2. no, 3. no, 4. no, 5. yes, 6. no, 7. yes.

Part III.

8. Attend to observable behavior.
9. Define limits of acceptable behavior and communicate these to your class.
10. Do not reward undesired behavior.
11. Avoid punishing undesired behaviors.
12. Provide an acceptable alternative student response for undesired behavior.
13. Reward appropriate behaviors.